HEAR
ME
ROAR

Published By:

www.PromotingNaturalHealth.com

HEAR ME ROAR

Hear Me Roar:

How to Defend Your Mind, Body and Heart Against People Who Suck

By Jennifer Cassetta and Lindsey Smith

Copyright © 2014 by Jennifer Cassetta and Lindsey Smith

The content of this book is for general instruction only. Each person's physical and emotional condition is unique. The instruction in this book is not intended to replace or interrupt the reader's relationship with a physician or other professional. Please consult your doctor for matters pertaining to your specific health and diet.

To contact the publisher, visit
www.PromotingNaturalHealth.com

Printed in the United States of America

ISBN-10: 0990646203
ISBN-13: 978-0-9906462-0-4

*We **dedicate** this to girls **everywhere.***
*Remember, you are **POWERFUL** beyond measure.*

CONTENTS

GRATITUDE

From Jennifer:

To Mom and Dad - thank you for instilling confidence in me at an early age, for your unconditional love and for being supportive of all of my dreams. To Julia and Anthony, thanks for always having my back. I love your guts!

Thank you to all of my friends and teachers at the World Martial Arts Center in NYC. Special thanks to all of my women warrior mentors for making strong look fabulous. To the long lineage of our teachers, the lifelong lessons learned from this school over my 10 years of training are worth its weight in gold - a deep bow to you all.

Thank you to Joshua Rosenthal for your coaching and having a vision to make this world a healthier and happier place!

Thank you to my man, Lindsay, for your steadfast love and support.

And major props to my writing partner, Lindsey, whom without this book would not exist! You're my inspiration.

From Lindsey:

To my parents—thanks for believing in my dreams and teaching me self-respect early on. I am forever grateful.

Joshua & Alex—one conversation really did change my life (and now, hopefully the lives of others). Thank you for believing in me.

Derek—thanks for totally not sucking and being supportive through it all. I love you.

Amie—as always, you go the extra mile to make a product shine. Thanks for being a part of this project!

Jenn—thanks for teaching me how to kick-ass in life, business and with this book!

From Jennifer & Lindsey:

Thanks to the amazing women who contributed to this book:

Amie Olson

Aire Plitcha

Alexandra Franzen

Akirah Robinson

Sheila B.

Maria B.

INTRODUCTION

Have you ever felt scared and completely powerless in a situation? We know we have, and chances are you have too. It breaks our hearts to hear stories of women in the US and around the world who have been taken advantage of, either physically or emotionally.

According to statistics, one in three women across the globe will be the victim of a sexual assault in their lifetime. That doesn't include all of the girls and women who have been abused in some horrific way and have never come forward to report it. It happens to your neighbors and your friends. It happens to even the most successful and confident people. Many celebrities have come out with their stories of sexual assault including Oprah, Ashley Judd, Teri Hatcher, Maya Angelou, Queen Latifah, Tori Amos, Mary J. Blige, Madonna, Julianne Hough, and Marilyn Monroe, who was one of the first women to speak publicly about it.

Perhaps you have been a victim of some horrible abuse. At the very least, we hope you no longer have to feel alone. At best, we wish you peace in your healing journey and hope you can then take the tools you learn in this book and help to empower and protect other women and girls in your life.

Maybe you have never experienced a sexual assault or any type of emotional or physical abuse. After reading this book, you will have the tools to stay confident and safe should you find yourself in a bad situation!

In addition to writing this book to keep young women stronger and safer, we also want to create a space for this conversation. Look for #HearMeRoar at the end of every section and get involved in the conversation through social media.

OUR STORIES

Here are the stories that helped change our attitude towards our personal safety, our power, and the word victim.

Jennifer's Story

I was twenty-four years old when some guy who sucks grabbed my ass (and whole package) on the street one night. It was 3 a.m. and I was coming home from a party in NYC. And yeah, I was pretty tipsy. Instead of practicing my street smarts and heading straight from the cab to my door, I took out my cell phone to listen to a voicemail.

After the initial moment of shock, I screamed, cursed, and spat fire his way until he took off down the street. As I called 911, I simultaneously took off after him in my stilettos hoping to catch the creep and hand him a can of whoop ass. But, lucky for him (and me) I didn't catch him.

The aftermath was actually the scariest part. What if I hadn't been able to scare him off? What if he had knocked me out, dragged me into a car, and taken me to some lair of danger? What if…what if?

This is where the powerful part comes in. I decided to get more serious about my Hapkido training. My three days a week at the dojang (martial arts studio) turned into six, and my routine continued for years this way until I actually made martial arts training and personal training my full-time career.

That night I didn't have to use any of the kick-ass techniques that my martial arts master taught me, except one very powerful lesson that changed my whole perception. Are you ready for it? Here goes:

If you ever feel backed into a corner and physically threatened, think like an animal in the wild. Become the tiger. Become the attacker and you no longer have to defend yourself. You then attack until your opponent becomes…dinner.

Lindsey's Story

When I was seventeen, I was a good girl. I was captain of the cheerleading squad, class president, and homecoming queen. You could say I had my stuff together.

Despite my good girl tendencies, I decided to go to a party with a friend from high school even though my inner voice was telling me not to go. Upon arrival I was handed a drink and thought, "Hey, why not?" A few sips in and I started to feel really weird.

The next thing I recall is waking up naked in a bed that wasn't mine. The unthinkable and unimaginable happened—I was date raped at a party by some guy who sucks.

As you can imagine, this completely affected my life. Everything from my relationships to my self-esteem to my confidence was completely tarnished. I felt powerless, broken, and ashamed.

It took a long time to reach the point of being a victor and no longer a victim, to accept myself rather than hate myself, and to realize it was not my fault.

In doing so, I've felt called and empowered to help other women like YOU feel confident in their skin, create their boundaries, and make decisions that can save their lives and cut out people who suck.

WHY WE CREATED THIS BOOK

Can you believe these statistics?!

- Every 2 minutes, someone in the US is sexually assaulted.
- 80% of sexual assault victims are under age 30.
- College age women are 4 times more likely to be victims of sexual assault.
- Women between the ages of 16 and 24 are four times more likely to be date raped than any other age group...and this is just from those who report an incident. This doesn't include the countless others who remain silent about their abuse.

We understand that sexual assault can happen to anyone and by anyone—regardless of gender, socioeconomic background, age, location, or sexual preference.

There has been male on male abuse, female on female abuse, and female on male abuse, but the majority is male on female abuse. And this is what our book is addressing.

We created this book to encourage YOU to be the confident and powerful woman you are in ALL areas of your life! And together, we can raise awareness and decrease these statistics.

*So let's **ROAR** together
and **stand tall** in our power,
and release our inner **she-beasts**!*

HOW TO USE THIS BOOK

This book is set up in three sections.

1. **Self-Confidence:** This sets the foundation for the book. We believe that being self-confident is more than feeling good—it is the foundation of your very being. Everyone deserves to feel confident and safe in their own skin.

2. **Safety:** Next, we talk about tools to keep you safe on dates, walking home, online, and everywhere in between. Personal safety is so much more than learning self-defense. It starts with your mind.

3. **Foods:** And to wrap it up, this section focuses on nourishing the body confidently and directly through mood-boosting foods and recipes that make you feel grounded and energized. These work to keep you safe from the inside out.

Each section includes inspiration, activities, and tools to use so you can successfully defend your mind, body, and heart against people who suck!

PEOPLE WHO SUCK

When we say "people who suck," we aren't only talking about predators and rapists, but also people who make you feel powerless or try to put you down.

Here are some examples of other people who suck (at least one of us has experienced something on this list):

The guy who grabbed your ass at a club

The friend who texts you negative shit constantly

The guy who stole your cab even though you were waiting there first

Your first boss who worked you to death and never thanked you

The crabby teacher who screamed at you when it wasn't your fault

The boyfriend who cheated on you

The guy that broke your heart

The creepy man who touched you inappropriately when you were a kid

The mean girl in high school who wouldn't let you in the "in crowd"

Sucky people are bound to come into your life, but this book will equip you with the tools to no longer allow them to suck the life out of you.

Let's get started!

SECTION 1
SELF-CONFIDENCE

"Because one *believes* in oneself,
one doesn't try to convince others.

Because one is *content* with oneself,
one doesn't need others' approval.

Because one *accepts* oneself,
the whole world accepts him or her."

- Lao Tzu

WHAT IS SELF-CONFIDENCE?

Let's Define Self-Confidence

The dictionary definition of confidence is to feel that you can succeed or do something well. So self-confidence means the feeling of success you find within yourself.

Hear Me Roar's definition of self-confidence is the belief that you hold all the power to stand strong in your worth and be yourself without judgment.

We believe self-confidence is an act of being. You showing up and standing firmly in who you are naturally makes you a confident woman.

And confident women are less likely to be a prey to people who suck.

Why Self-Confidence Is Key!

Confidence is something we are naturally born with. Let's face it, babies and children aren't afraid to act without care and just be themselves.

But then, life happens. And as we grow up, we are fed lies. Or as we like to call it, confidence hacking. People hack our confidence by feeding us lies like:

"Girls aren't meant to play sports."

"You aren't good enough for that."

"You are too fat to fit into that dress."

"You should have smaller thighs."

"You should look like this super star or else you are worthless."

"Quit being yourself and be more of who this person is."

…and the list goes on.

These lies have been enough to rip our self-esteem and completely diminish any self-confidence that we once had.

But teaching self-confidence is less about teaching and more about the unlearning of lies we've been told since we were little girls. Stepping up and reclaiming our worth is a journey worth starting now. In the next few sections, we'll map out tools and techniques to help you unlearn old habits and relearn positive ones.

Let's take back our self-confidence once and for all.

On a scale of 1-10, how confident do you feel today?
#HearMeRoar

CHOOSING CONFIDENCE

"Change the way you look at things
and *the things* you look at *change."*

- Wayne Dyer

Choose Your Words

Are you constantly beating yourself up? Maybe you smack talk yourself—everything from your hair to your stomach to your thighs?

Confident people don't have time for BS thoughts and words.

It's important to choose words and phrases throughout the day that lift you up as opposed to tear you down.

Take notice of how you talk to yourself on a daily basis. If you find yourself saying more negative things than positive things, simply create three positive things you like about yourself or even a fun mantra to keep with you. Then, every time you find yourself talking smack on your body, you can flip the script.

Hear Me Roar Confidence Booster:

This next week, focus on only using words or sayings that lift you up. You can do this both verbally and mentally.

Here are three things I absolutely love (or at least like right now) about myself:

1.

2.

3.

Here is a list of uplifting mantras you can repeat to yourself when your self-talk goes sour:

I am powerful beyond measure.

I am worthy of self-love.

I like myself.

I am strong and powerful.

Or you can create your own here:

_____

_____

_____

_____

_____

_____

What's your personal mantra?
#HearMeRoar

Tweet Now:
Say nice things to yourself. Your future self will thank you.
#HearMeRoar

How Are You Speaking To Others?

Now check yourself again. How are you speaking to others? Are you lifting them up? Are you bitching about them behind their back? Are you encouraging, or are you a Negative Nancy?

Throughout the day, notice your words, your thoughts, and your actions towards others.

Self-confident people tend to look for the good and encourage others. If you find yourself putting people down more than lifting them up, try this simple exercise to help get you into the positive mindset.

Hear Me Roar Confidence Booster:

Today, write a thank you letter to someone in your life, really uplifting them and praising their strengths.

OR you can go the extra mile and write a praise letter to someone you may have put down in the past.

Note: You don't actually have to GIVE the letter to them, but this simple act can switch your thinking from negative to uplifting in a matter of minutes.

HMR

Dear

Love,

Let's Hear From You:
How often do you lift other people up?
#HearMeRoar

Tweet Now:
Be nice to others. It's good karma.
#HearMeRoar

Drop Comparisons

"Comparison is the thief of joy."
– Eleanor Roosevelt

It's super easy to get caught up on social media, blogs, and photo-shopped magazine spreads.

According to the National Association of Anorexia Nervosa and Associated Disorders, about seventy percent of girls grades five through twelve said magazine images influence their ideas of a perfect body.

Comparisons kill. The moment we compare is the moment we lose a sense of our own self-worth.

Let's face it—no one's life is as glamorous as they put online. Of course, we all want to put our best selfies and fun times out there. But that's not actually reality one hundred percent of the time.

Even the women in the magazines don't actually look

like that. They are stretched, cropped, tweaked, tanned and plumped to look like unrealistic and unattainable standards of beauty.

In the real world, sometimes we have off days. Our face breaks out or we feel bloated. We get sad, vulnerable, hurt and depressed. We're all human.

Of course, we probably aren't going to post a picture of us crying to let everyone know we are sad. But, we have to understand the deeper picture here. We are all humans with pretty complex issues and completely bio-individual design. We all have flaws and all get hurt. We mess up.

And the thing is—EVERYONE does.

So the next time you find yourself in the dangerous comparison cycle, recognize that life is a journey, not a race or a destination. Cut yourself some slack and drop the comparisons.

Let's Hear From You:
Are you ready to drop the comparisons? If so, how?
#HearMeRoar

Tweet Now:
Drop the comparisons and embrace who you are.
#HearMeRoar

Step Into Your Light

Speaking of comparisons, is there anyone in your life that

you just kind of hate? Maybe for no reason? It could include some comparison, but maybe not. There is just something about that person that you can't stand?

Chances are you are really seeing a mirror reflection of something in yourself. Maybe it's something you aren't digging about yourself, or maybe it's a success that you wish you had.

Many times when we are annoyed with someone, there is actually something in them that we don't like or that we admire or wish to be like. This may turn into us hating this person or feeling jealous.

It's important to recognize these feelings and ask yourself the deeper question, "Why am I saying these things or feeling this way about this person?" Get real with yourself and answer the deeper question.

The light we see in others and the success we see in others is meant to show us that it is possible for us, too.

Step into your light. We can all shine brightly with our unique gifts. We all have unique gifts. It doesn't mean you have to sit on the sidelines anymore. Show up to your light and own up to your worth!

Let's Hear From You:
Are you ready to step into your light? If so, how?
#HearMeRoar

Tweet Now:
Step into your own light. Own your worth.
#HearMeRoar

Focus On Your Strengths

Chances are, you are really good at something. Or maybe you are good at a lot of things.

Are you good at math? Maybe tennis is your thing? Jenn is bad-ass in martial arts while Lindsey can make up freestyle raps about kale. (Hey, we didn't say they had to be resume worthy, just what makes you unique.)

Hear Me Roar Confidence Booster

Whatever those things are, let's highlight some of your strengths!

My top 5 strengths as a woman are:

1.

2.

3.

4.

5.

It's normal to doubt ourselves and think we are aren't good enough. Keep these strengths somewhere close and remember them when you start to doubt yourself.

Let's Hear From You!
What's one of your unique strengths?
#HearMeRoar

Tweet now:
When in doubt, recall your strengths.
#HearMeRoar

Choose Your Response

You can't always choose the situation or circumstance, but you can choose how you respond.

Of course there are those times when life is just frustrating.

Sometimes, it's completely okay to scream f-bombs in your head for five minutes, then take a deep breath and release the tension.

Other times, it's choosing to respond in a positive way. Sure, you COULD bitch the telemarketer out on the phone. BUT, should you? How will this change your life or the scenario?

Try this simple FUN formula the next time you are in a complex or frustrating situation:

F – Feel the emotions. It's important to take time to feel your emotions. Don't completely negate them or respond immediately. Take five minutes to feel. Sometimes this can include crying. Sometimes it can be screaming f-bombs in your head or your car. Take five, breathe, and let yourself feel.

U – Understand the situation. Next, understand what's really going on. What's the cause of your frustration or pain? Is someone messing with your flow? Do you have things you need to do and feel you can't waste time on the phone? Once you understand the situation, think of the bigger picture. Is this ten minutes on the phone REALLY going to mess with my entire day? Really understand the entirety of the situation itself.

N – Now, respond with love. Now, choose to respond from your heart more than your head. Once you feel more relaxed and can understand the big picture of the situation, you can then CHOOSE to respond with a loving heart rather than a hateful head. Those five minutes can truly make all the difference.

Let's Hear From You!
Have you tried taking five to feel your emotions?
How did it work for you?
#HearMeRoar

Tweet Now:
Choose to respond with a loving heart
rather than a hateful head!
#HearMeRoar

BODY CONFIDENCE

Check it! Your body is f'ing amazing!

It breathes without reminders to do so.

It beats a heartbeat to keep you alive.

It heals even the deepest wounds.

It grows your hair back from a bad haircut.

It energizes you to run, play and laugh.

It feels, deeply and intimately.

It protects you from outside harm.

It digests food to keep you sustained all day long.

It even digests junk food.

So let's face it—your body is a magical machine that is constantly working for you and through you.

While you've been shaming your body in the bathroom mirror or smack-talking your thighs to a friend, your body has actually been doing everything in its power to save you, nourish you, protect you and keep you alive.

It literally fights for your life, every single day.

So the next time you catch yourself about to talk shit on your body, express gratitude for all the daily things your body is doing to keep you breathing and your heart beating.

And then you will realize why there is absolutely nothing wrong with you or your body.

Tweet Now:
There is absolutely nothing wrong with your body.
#HearMeRoar

Apology Letter To Your Body

So now that we have the facts straight about your body (yeah, we know, it totally rocks!), it's time for YOU to stand up and write your body an apology letter and then a love letter.

Don't worry; we created this super simple mad-libs style letter to make it easy peasy lemon squeezy. Or just plain simple. You get it!

Dear body,

I'm so, so, so sorry that I _____ you for so long.

I didn't mean to call you names like _____ and _____.

I only said that out of fear and shame.

I deeply appreciate you for getting me through _____.

I love you with all my heart (literally).

xoxo,

_____

Ahhhhh…doesn't that feel better already? Okay, now it's time to write a love letter to your body. Tell it all the amazing things it does for you.

Love Letter To Your Body

Dear body,

WOW! You are an incredible _____.

I cannot believe that you _____, _____ and still _____.

I also love your _____. In fact there are SO many things I love about you, I can't keep track.

I love you and thank you for loving me back.

xoxo,

_____

PS Extra love for my _____. It's my favorite thing about me!

HEAR ME ROAR

Let's Hear From You!
What do you appreciate most about what
your body does for you?
#HearMeRoar

Tweet Now:
Your body is a miracle. Appreciate it.
#HearMeRoar

Exercises To Love Your Body More

While writing a love letter to your body is a GREAT practice, there are other things you can do (even on a daily basis) to show your body that you love and care about it.

The next few exercises are designed to give you some prompts, tips, and pointers on how to practice the art of self-care and self-love.

Again, please remember that everyone is bio-individual. So what works for one person may not work for the next. Try some of the exercises to see which best resonate with you and make them daily habits. If something else feels right and helps you love your body more, then do that. There is no cookie-cutter approach here.

Throw Out The Scale

"My beauty is not **defined** by a # on a scale."

Oh the dreaded scale. A scale tends to remind us of a specific number that we once saw. Maybe it was the lowest we ever weighed, or a number we are currently striving for—either way, the scale can be terrifying.

Often times, we look to the scale to give us satisfaction—that our body is good enough. That we finally reached a goal and feel like we have arrived in our perfect health condition.

However, the scale really tells you none of that. It doesn't tell your body make-up, your health markers, or your unique shape. It certainly doesn't tell you about your genetic make-up or capabilities. And it definitely is not an indication of your self-worth and true beauty.

So why do we waste so much time obsessing over one single number?

Instead, focus on how you feel—physically, emotionally and socially. Let the emphasis be on your HEALTH and HAPPINESS, not a mere number.

Feel free to have a scale releasing party with you and your girlfriends. Make a pact to not let a scale define you anymore. Throw the scales away, embrace your unique beauty, and focus on your health and how you feel on the inside!

Tweet Now:
Beauty is not defined by a number on a scale.
#HearMeRoar

Celebrate Your Successes

So you passed an exam? You decided to brush your teeth today? Damn, girl! Celebrate those successes. No matter how large or small—celebrate your successes every day.

A great way to do this is to start a "success jar." Simply decorate a jar, write a daily success on a slip of paper, and drop it in! Days when you are feeling extremely low, reach into the jar and pull out a success. Remember all the things you ARE doing and HAVE done to keep you going. Even the smallest thing can be the biggest success.

Let's Hear From You!
What's one of your successes today?
#HearMeRoar

Tweet Now:
Celebrate your successes every single day.
#HearMeRoar

Go Make-up Free For One Day A Week

Do you remember the first time you put on make-up? Most girls start experimenting with make-up early on and then re-introduce it in middle school.

Over time, make-up can eventually become a way of life and something we think we HAVE to do in order to feel attractive and beautiful.

Sure, sometimes make-up can be fun. Sometimes wearing make-up can truly be an artistic expression of who we are, but it should NOT be used as a means to define our self-worth and beauty.

Taking the make-up free challenge can totally help you feel more connected and comfortable in your skin than ever before. By looking at your face in the mirror without make-up and going into public spaces shedding your truth, you can learn a lot about yourself.

At first, it MAY feel uncomfortable. It may feel like you are baring your entire soul. You may even feel naked or weird.

However, try it just once a week and then go from there.

Over time, you might find that you truly appreciate your skin and your beauty that was there all along—you just spent the past several years trying to cover it up.

Below is a make-up free guide to help you feel more confident in your own skin.

Start off make-up minimum. What can you do without? Maybe just foundation and mascara would be a minimalist way to start? Great! Work your way down until you can bare all!

Give your skin a breather! By giving your skin a break from make-up, you are actually helping it breathe and rejuvenate. Make it a habit to take off your make-up at the end of every day. Make-up free days will also give your skin an extra boost!

Get your rest! Sleep is crucial for skin health! When you sleep at night, there is an internal cleaning crew going through your body, balancing your hormones and making sure you are in check! So if your skin is breaking out or if you are getting dark circles under your eyes, try getting some more shut-eye, not more concealer!

Meditate. Breathing and simple meditations can help relax your mind AND your body. (Yes, your skin included!)

Exercise. Exercise helps release toxins from the body by sweating out all the bad stuff. Through this, your skin naturally releases build-up as well.

Let's Hear From You!
Show us your best make-up free selfie!
#HearMeRoar

Tweet Now:
Stop concealing your natural beauty. Let it shine!
#HearMeRoar

Take Back Your Time

A typical woman spends approximately 136 days, 3,736 hours, 223,560 minutes and over thirteen million seconds getting ready in her lifetime. This includes everything from putting on make-up and fake eyelashes to getting spray tanned.

If you find yourself "getting ready" for the sake of getting ready or doing some sort of beauty regime to appease everyone but yourself, we encourage you to take back your time!

And we ask you, "What if you spent less time getting ready and more time showing up to life?"

What would you do with that time you get back?

What would you create?

Who would you become?

What fun would you have?

How can you take back your getting ready time this week? Make a list of some things you want to do with the time you are taking back.

Example: Learn to play the piano, read a book, write a book, or go for a run.

1.

2.

3.

4.

5.

Let's Hear From You!
How are you taking back your time this week?
#Hear Me Roar

Tweet Now:
Spend less time getting ready and more time showing up.
#HearMeRoar

Body Love Meditation

Next time you lash out at your body in fear or anger, practice this mini-meditation instead.

This will help you learn to love every inch, every freckle, and every part of your being.

Start by planting your feet firmly on the floor. Sit upright or in a comfortable position that works for you.

Now breathe deeply in through your nose and out through your mouth. And again, in through your nose and out through your mouth.

Now gently and slowly rub your hands together, really feeling your skin.

Feel the texture—the smooth areas, the rough patches. Take notice of what you feel.

Now breathe in through your nose and out through your mouth.

Appreciate your skin for covering you and projecting you.

Wiggle your hands and your feet. Thank them for helping you move and doing what you need them to do.

Now, place your hand on your heart. Feel the beats. Slowly breathe in and breathe out. Notice your breath, notice your heartbeats.

Give thanks to your body for nourishing you with oxygen.

Take a moment now to consider your thoughts and ideas about your own body. How are you feeling right now, thinking about your body image? Do you feel content, comfortable, uncomfortable, happy, sad, angry, afraid, or mad? Maybe you feel a combination? It's okay to feel these ways.

Now ask yourself, "What if I accepted my body just as it is?" "What if I could feel okay with my entire body?" Imagine what that would feel like for you.

Think about a time when you accepted your body, either your whole body or a part of your body. Which parts were the easiest to accept?

Take a few more deep breaths in through your nose and out through your mouth.

As you breathe, send loving thoughts from your heart to each area of your body. With every inhale, imagine your body receiving this love and becoming lighter and healthier. With every exhale, continue to send loving thoughts throughout your body and imagine your heart expanding.

Do this for several more breaths, receiving love with every inhale, and sending more love to your body with every exhale… receiving love with every inhale and sending love with every exhale…receiving love and sending love.

Now slowly breathe in and out one last time.

Appreciate yourself for taking the time to love your body just the way it is.

Let's Hear From You!
What did you take away from the Body Love Meditation?
#HearMeRoar

Tweet Now:
Slow down and appreciate all your body does for you.
#HearMeRoar

CONFIDENCE & BEYOND

Lift Up Other Women

In order to make a change with beauty standards and definitions—it actually starts with us. It starts with our relationship with one another.

Women need to come together and lift one another up rather than tear one another down.

We know that organizations and women's groups can be cliquey at times. Sometimes there is a competition and a "we are better than you" mentality that follows. However, it only takes one person taking a stance to break down the walls and accept our fellow women.

Let's just start being nicer to each other, okay? Here are some ways to be nicer to our fellow women:

- Write an encouraging note to a gal in class.

- Ask someone who looks a little lonely to get some coffee/tea after class.

- Write a thank-you note to a woman in your life who deserves it.

- Get involved globally. Right now, there are many women in mainstream media standing up for one another. Join the cause and stand up for women everywhere.

- Get a female mentor. Learn from a woman you admire.

- And then, when you feel ready, BE the mentor to a younger gal!

Let's Hear From You!
What ways are you lifting up other women in your life?
#HearMeRoar

Tweet Now:
Hey women—let's start lifting each other up
rather than tearing each other down!
#HearMeRoar

Increase Your Fun!

Many times, we are so goal oriented and success focused, we forget to stop and enjoy life. Adding fun into your daily routine can help decrease stress, increase your focus and give your happiness a boost.

For you, fun may look like reading a romance novel or maybe going on a hike. For others, it may look like going Salsa dancing with the girls or going out for a fancy dinner. Whatever feels like fun to you—do that! This is especially helpful during stressful times like finals week.

List a few FUN things YOU can do when times get tense:

1.

2.

3.

4.

5.

Let's Hear From You!
What fun are you adding into your life this week?
#HearMeRoar

Tweet Now:
Making time for fun can also increase productivity!
#HearMeRoar

An Attitude Of Gratitude

Focusing on what you are grateful for can reduce your stress and anxiety by up to eighty percent. So many times we complain about what's wrong or what we don't have that we forget to see all the amazing things we can be grateful for—like running water, food to eat, your beating heart, and friends and family. An attitude of gratitude can go a long way to increase your happiness and balance your hormones.

Take the gratitude challenge for the next week! At the

beginning or end of the day, write down three to five things you are grateful for! Do you notice a shift?

Use the guided journal below to help you!

Day 1: Focus on family. What or who are you grateful for?

Today, I am grateful for:

_____

_____

_____

_____

Day 2: Focus on friends. What or who are you grateful for?

Today, I am grateful for:

_____

_____

_____

_____

Day 3: Focus on people. What or who are you grateful for?

Today, I am grateful for:

_____

_____

_____

_____

Day 4: Focus on school or work. What are you grateful for?

Today, I am grateful for:

_____

_____

_____

_____

Day 5: Focus on your body. What are you grateful for?

Today, I am grateful for:

_____

_____

_____

_____

Day 6: Focus on fun! What are you grateful for?

Today, I am grateful for:

_____

_____

_____

_____

Day 7: Focus on the simple things. What are you grateful for?

Today, I am grateful for:

_____

_____

_____

_____

HEAR
ME
ROAR

Let's Hear From You!
Did you take the gratitude challenge?
Let us know your experience!
#HearMeRoar

Tweet Now:
Today, I am grateful for _____.
#HearMeRoar

Body Shifts For Energy Shifts

These simple yoga poses are great for a wide range of feelings and emotions you may be carrying with you. Sometimes, shifting your body is enough to shift your energy!

These poses are broken down by an emotion or feeling you may experience. Use them as necessary or make them a part of your daily practice.

Anxiety: Cat/Cow

Yep, this yoga pose is exactly what you envision. Start by coming onto all fours with your wrists underneath your shoulders and your knees hip-width apart. As you inhale, drop your stomach toward the ground, allow your back to curve downward, and raise your head. This is cow pose. Then exhale and round your back like a cat. Repeat this pose several times with each breath. You can even repeat a mantra like, "I am letting go of what no longer serves me."

Depression: Tree Pose

This pose keeps you rooted just like a tree. It can help you feel grounded and in the present moment. Stand firmly with your feet planted and spread your feet hip distance apart. Slowly lift your left foot up off the ground, balancing your weight on your right foot. Bend your left knee and point out towards the side. Use your left hand to grasp for your left ankle. Draw your left foot up and place the sole of your foot on your inner thigh with your toes pointing to the floor. Gaze forward with your hands at heart center or take your gaze up and lift your hands up high above your head in a "V" position.

Broken Heart/Ready for Love: Standing Reach

Stand tall with the bases of your big toes touching. Lengthen your tailbone and stand tall with your palms facing up and have your hands form a "V" shape by your sides.

Energy: Downward Facing Dog

Start by coming on to all fours with your wrists underneath your shoulders and your knees hip-width apart. Spread your palms and turn your toes under. Exhale and lift your knees away from the floor, lengthening your tailbone and slightly bending your knees. Keep lengthening your spine and push your top thighs back. Stretch your heels down or towards the floor.

Self-Confidence: Feel confident in your warrior positions!

It's no surprise that the Warrior poses in yoga are directly related to our self-confidence. After all, these poses make you feel strong, focused, and hyper aware of your body.

Warrior I

For Warrior I, start by standing in Mountain Pose, with your feet planted firmly, hips distance apart and arms down by your side. Step one foot back and form a short stance with your heels evenly aligned. Bend your front knee and straighten your back leg, turning your toes slightly forward. Square your hips and shoulders to the front of the mat and raise your arms to the sky.

Warrior II

From Warrior I, keep your heels aligned as you open up your hips and shoulders towards the side of the room. Extend your arms parallel to the floor, reaching out in opposite directions. Keep your front leg bent slightly and you back leg straight, making sure your hips are facing the side. Take your gaze to the top of your front hand looking forward.

Cravings: Seated Meditation

Find a seated position with your legs crossed at your knees that feels comfortable for you. Close your eyes and slowly breathe in and out. Extend your hands above your head in a "V" position and repeat, "I release all that hinders my growth."

Body Love: Mountain Pose

Stand tall with the bases of your big toes touching. Lengthen your tailbone and stand tall with your arms down by your side and palms facing out. Take a few deep breaths. Repeat to yourself, "I completely love and accept myself, just as I am."

Let's Hear From You!
What's your favorite yoga pose and why?
#HearMeRoar

Tweet Now:
Shifting your body can also shift your energy.
#HearMeRoar

When All Else Fails—Dance!

Our motto is—if you are in a funk—get funky! Dancing is a great way to instantly boost your happiness and release negative or toxic energy.

So put on your favorite dance tune and get the party started!

Aren't sure what to play? We made this funkalicious playlist just for you! All these songs were hand selected (with love) due to their fun beats and female empowerment lyrics!

Hear Me Roar Playlist

1. "Roar" by Katy Perry

2. "Respect" by Aretha Franklin

3. "I Will Survive" by Gloria Gaynor

4. "Flawless" by Beyonce

5. "Try" by Colbie Caillat

6. "Fighter" by Christina Aguilera

7. "Survivor" by Destiny's Child

8. "You Gotta Be" by Des'ree

9. "Video" by India Arie

10. "You Learn" by Alanis Morissette

Let's Hear From You!
What's your favorite empowering dance tune?
#HearMeRoar

Tweet Now:
When all else fails—dance!
#HearMeRoar

SET YOUR STANDARDS

Define Your Non-Negotiables

Creating non-negotiables is a great way to create boundaries for people who enter your life from dating relationships to friendships.

For example, if you know you want to live a drug-free life, then for your dating life, it's important to date someone who is also drug-free. That is a non-negotiable.

This immediately sets boundaries and eliminates potential sucky people from entering your life. Ain't nobody got time for that.

And after all, you choose who gets to stay in your life.

What are your non-negotiables? Write them in each category below. Remember, they can overlap.

Examples:

Category	Non-negotiables
Work relationships	Being appreciated & respected
Friendships	Being respected & heard
Dating Relationships	Non-smoker, great listener, kind to my family

Your Turn:

Category	Non-negotiables
Work relationships	
Friendships	
Dating Relationships	

Note: If at ANYTIME you feel uncomfortable in a situation or are feeling doubt in a relationship, go back and check out your non-negotiables and remember to honor yourself and your values.

Tweet Now:
I define my standards.
#HearMeRoar

Dress With Confidence

Dressing with confidence is less about adhering to the latest fashion trends and more about feeling good about what you are wearing and being self-assured in all situations.

For many people, feeling more confident can simply be switching out some sweats for jeans. For others, it's learning to dress to your body type and unique shape. It's also important to notice how to dress for your audience.

Here is a simple guide from our friend and stylist, Aire Plitcha. We love Aire because she truly encompasses self-confidence with her own style and helps other women do the same. She made us realize that it's less about the fashion statement and labels and more about how you feel in what you are wearing.

Here is Aire's super simple style guide to get you feeling like the confident chick you are:

Have one go-to style or silhouette. Wear something that makes you feel like you can conquer the world! We all have a pair of shoes, dress, or in my case sequins that we can put on and automatically feel ready to start the day in style! If you're reading this and thinking that you do not have this, stop what you're doing and figure out what this could be for you. I recommend to my clients to go back to their childhood and think of the piece that they hated taking off and find a way to bring that to your adult life. If you loved playing dress up and wearing that Cinderella crown, try a new sparkly headband. I'm confident this will work for you.

Wear color. Color, even in the form of an accessory, is an easy way to refresh pieces you've had for a long time. It also helps you appear happier and more open to embracing the world. Once you see the response, I bet you'll be in more color before you know it.

Accessorize. Sometimes the item in your wardrobe that makes you feel like you can take on the world comes in the form of a shoe, bag, or scarf. I always say figure out what it is about that piece that makes you feel so great and try to mimic it in a bigger way. Accessories are a great way to refresh any item, help you go from day to night, or change the whole aesthetic of a look. Don't be shy when it comes to building up this part of your closet!

Sometimes less is less. This is especially true when it comes to trends! Just because all of your girlfriends are wearing the latest item doesn't mean you have to. Not every trend works for every person's style or bank account. If you're determined to try it, figure out a way you can work a version of the trend into your wardrobe without breaking the bank on a style that will end up sitting in your closet.

Let's Hear From You!
What's your confidence outfit?
#HearMeRoar

Tweet Now:
I'm ditching the trends and focusing on feeling good!
#HearMeRoar

"Fit Out"

Rather than trying to fit in all the time, focus on fitting out. Sometimes the most badass thing to do is NOT doing what everyone else is doing. Sure, it's normal to want to fit in with people that we think are cool and doing cool things. However, keep in mind that fitting out can often lead to a better understanding of who you are and what you stand for.

Here are three warning signs that you should really be fitting out:

1. **You feel guilty.** You should never feel guilty about doing or not doing something. If you find you are guilt ridden, protect yourself early on by standing up for yourself or getting yourself out of the situation.

2. **You feel pressured.** If you ever feel pressured into doing something that you aren't sure about (drugs, alcohol, sex,

cheating, eating, etc)—make sure to set the boundary NOW. If people are your friends and if they truly respect you, they will totally be cool with whatever decision you make. They will think the version of you that said, "No," is just as cool as if you said, "Yes."

3. **It doesn't mesh with your personal value system.** We talked about our personal value systems earlier in this chapter. So this is a good guideline on how to check yourself in situations. Don't let someone else's value system run yours. Always check in with your own!

Tweet Now:
I stand strong in my body.
#HearMeRoar

Lead By Example

Don't wait until you get named class president or event co-chair to stand up and act like a leader. Let out your biggest ROAR by example NOW! You have the power!

Remember that people relate through experiences and look up to people who run in the same social circles they do.

Here are three simple ways to show up and act like a leader in your life NOW:

1. **Watch your words.** While actions speak louder than words, the truth is—words can still cut deeply. I mean, we can all probably recall a time from childhood where someone said something mean to us. And sometimes, it still hurts. Watch the words you say to people from here on out, especially when it comes to team work or group work. Praise others for a good job and give constructive feedback when necessary.

2. **Take responsibility for your actions.** (Yes, this means when you mess up, too!) Many times we use excuses as to why we did or didn't do something right. Like maybe you got a C on a test and you said, "The teacher didn't grade fairly." Or maybe you were up for a job promotion but didn't get it, and you immediately blamed the bad management. In both of these situations, they are just mere excuses. Instead of making excuses, take responsibility. Sure, you didn't want to get a C, but if you own up and take responsibility, it helps you step into being the leader you are and can help motivate you to do better next time.

3. **Manage your well-being.** Did you know that being an essential and effective leader means you need to take care of yourself? Yes! Wellness is a crucial step for leading by example NOW! By investing and taking care of yourself and your health, you have more energy to show up for projects, events, and people who need you!

Let's Hear From You!
How are you leading by example this week?
#HearMeRoar

Tweet Now:
Leaders don't wait until they are given a title to lead.
They do it now!
#HearMeRoar

CONFIDENTLY COMBAT PEOPLE WHO SUCK

How To Handle Energy Suckers

So we all know that one person in our life who is always complaining. They are like a vampire to your energy lifeline, just constantly sucking away at you! It feels like they literally want to suck you dry of everything and offer nothing in return.

Here are six ways to combat those energy suckers in your life:

1. **Don't give in to the negative talk.** Many times, these soul suckers want you to dig in and have a complete bitch fest with them. However, this totally messes with your own energy. So stand up and defend your energy! Don't give in to the negative downward spiral this person wants you to go on. Instead, combat them with your PMA. (That's street talk for "positive mental attitude"). Offer real and tangible solutions in a positive way for the person. But whatever you do—don't let yourself fall victim to their negativity. If you consistently do this, the person will eventually regcognize what you are trying to do and realize they can't bring you along to their pity party.

2. **Crowd out.** If this person really bothers you, but you can't escape, try only being around this person in a group setting. This way, you can have backup and "crowd out" some of the negativity by focusing on the other people in the group. This also gives you a chance to leave the situation without feeling badly because other people will be there to entertain.

3. **Talk about something light.** Chances are, if you start talking about school, work, boys, cliques, etc—the talk can get

pretty intense. Lighten the mood by mentioning a cute kitten you saw or a really nice note you received or sent to someone. Talking about lighter and more positive things can help switch the Negative Nancy into a Positive Peg. Okay, it might still take some time, but it can help you stay sane in the situation!

4. **Beware of your time.** So if this is something you truly can't escape, just be aware of how you spend your time with them. Maybe instead of planning an open-ended coffee/tea date, you instead suggest an activity that gets you moving and out by a certain time. This way, you can guard how much time you are spending with them to ensure that your energy isn't compromised!

5. **Block, hide or unfriend.** So maybe that energy vampire sits on Facebook. And every day, as your scroll down your news feed, there he or she is--sucking the energy out of you. Everything is negative. And everything is a drag. Don't let their negative attitude bring you down anymore. Simply block, hide, or unfriend them. This way you can ensure peace of mind and a better attitude while scrolling through your feed.

6. **If all else fails—send love from afar.** Sometimes there is absolutely nothing you can do to protect yourself from taking on the energy of a soul sucker. So in that case, the BEST thing you can do is release them from your life while sending them love from afar so you can continue living your life in a positive way.

Tweet Now:
When negative people are around,
crank up your positive vibes.
#HearMeRoar

CONFIDENTLY FORGIVE

Five Tools To Forgive People Who Suck

Yes, it's a lot easier to forgive the guy who cut in line at the grocery store than it is the guy who assaulted you. But finding forgiveness in all situations will help you become more powerful.

By no means are we suggesting that you need to invite these people back into your life. You don't need to call up your ex-boyfriend and tell him you've forgiven him and that you should get back together. You just need to start the healing process by forgiving him in your heart. Because when your heart becomes lighter, you become stronger and more confident.

1.   Forgiveness is good for your health. Holding onto resentment and pain is literally toxic for the body. By letting go and forgiving, you are choosing health for YOURSELF!

2.   Apology not needed. If you were assaulted, you are probably not going to ask your offender to send you an apology letter. Instead, you need accept the circumstance and find inner peace. A great way to find some inner healing is to seek compassion for all people (yes, even sucky ones). Connect with the basic human condition—we all suffer (in some form). From sickness to loneliness to anxiety to depression to sadness—we've all experienced suffering in some capacity. While finding a sense of compassion in any scenario can't change the past or prevent a sucky thing from happening, it CAN help you feel more compassion for fellow humans.

3.   Forgive yourself. It's easy to replay instances in our heads about the circumstances or situations. But it's important to

find forgiveness within you. Remember that we all make mistakes. By forgiving yourself, you can let go of personal and toxic resentment.

4. It's not your fault. A lot of the time, we blame ourselves for bad things people did to US! Never is it okay for someone to take advantage of you, your body, your energy, or your self-worth. Remember, that is NEVER okay! And it is NOT your fault!

5. To truly forgive is not to forget, but to release and find inner peace. Sure, you may get angry or upset. Sometimes triggers can pop up for you. But forgiveness is a constant process of letting go and releasing. Just know that this is a lifelong journey. Learning and practicing forgiveness is ongoing.

And remember—forgiveness doesn't excuse a sucky person's behavior at all! BUT it does help prevent your own heart from crippling.

Tweet Now:
Forgiveness is a tool of power and self-confidence,
not weakness!
#HearMeRoar

CONFIDENTLY YOU!

Be Genuine & Be You

As we mentioned at the beginning of this chapter, self-confidence has a lot to do with the unlearning of old belief patterns we were taught early on.

It's important to get back to basics and understand who you really are!

Many times, we lose sight of ourselves throughout our adulthood because we are busy trying to please everyone else or conform to societal pressures. But in order to become a rock star, we need to know our unique purpose and how we can contribute our kick-ass talents to the world.

Take a minute to tap into your genuine and confident self—one with no reserves and a heart full of love.

Ask yourself these questions:

Who am I?

What is my purpose?

How can I serve the world?

Now, take a minute to just write down anything that comes to your mind when you think of these questions:

_____

_____

_____

_____

_____

Let's Hear From You!
Tell us your rock star purpose!
#HearMeRoar

Tweet Now:
I have a rock star purpose and kick-ass talents
to give to the world.
#HearMeRoar

Your Self-Confidence Mantra:

Before we go into the next two sections of the book, let's create a personal mantra that you can carry with you on your journey. This should be something personal and based on where you are and where you want to go.

For example, if you want to focus on strength, your mantra can be, "I am strong and powerful."

Or maybe you want to focus on self-love. Your mantra can be, "I completely love and accept myself, just as I am."

Your turn! Write your personal mantra here:

_____

_____

_____

Let's Hear From You!
We want to hear your personal mantra! Share with us!
#HearMeRoar

Tweet Now:
You are strong. You are powerful. You are capable.
#HearMeRoar

SECTION 2
PERSONAL SAFETY

"To understand your fear is the beginning of really seeing."
– Bruce Lee

What Is Personal Safety?

Safety is the condition of being protected from danger, risk, or injury.

Therefore, personal safety means being able to protect yourself from danger, risk, or injury.

Personal safety is important for these three reasons:

1. Let's face it—sometimes someone who sucks may try to hurt you either emotionally or physically. Having the tools to defend yourself against people who suck will give you the power to avoid these situations in the first place. This helps create a safe space for you to live your life and follow your dreams.

2. Personal safety will also help you fight for yourself and your dreams when you need to.

3. The ability to protect yourself makes you feel like a badass.

    As you read this next section remember the following:

    • If you've been hurt in the past, emotionally or physically, learning these tools can help take your past experience and turn it into something powerful within you.
    • You may think that learning personal safety begins in a self-defense class at a gym. However, awareness increases our safety. Even reading the words in this next section and hearing the stories written here can help tap into your intuition which can help save your life.
    • Living safely doesn't mean living your life guarded and paranoid. It means living your life as a bad ass and being able to handle any danger, risk, or injury that may come your way.

Let's Hear From You!
What do you currently know about
personal safety and self-defense?
#HearMeRoar

Tweet Now:
In order to take on your dreams,
you'll need to conquer your fears first.
#HearMeRoar

SOCIAL SAFETY

We love social media! On a personal level it has kept us connected to friends we haven't seen in decades. We get to see friends who live across the globe get married, have babies, and accomplish amazing feats. We can be there for them when something sad happens.

Heck, we even met on social media!

So we all agree there are plenty of benefits of social media. But if you're not safe you may find yourself being stalked by someone who sucks.

Many women don't even realize they're being stalked or followed because the signs aren't so obvious. Your stalker hasn't followed you home from work and doesn't call you anonymously breathing heavily. Nowadays, stalkers can track you down by cyber stalking you. And it's a lot easier than you think!

We have a close friend who is an attractive, sassy TV host. Her fans love her. However, with lots of public media attention comes the risk of negative attention. She encountered a man who crossed the line from fan to stalker without her realizing it until she received his violent threats via email. He threatened to come to her home and kill her as well as her family and he knew exactly where she lived. But how?

After reporting the disturbing emails to the Los Angeles Police Department, the police were able to investigate the case and track down her stalker. It turns out he had found her private email and home address from the company that her website was registered with.

You don't have to be a celebrity to have a stalker. Here are some telltale signs that there may be someone watching you online:

• A stranger likes and comments on every single thing you post.

- The stranger often comments on how you look.
- The stranger has stupid usernames like MikeRotch1 or BallsForKicking.
- The stranger asks you out on a date.
- The stranger asks you for personal details about where you live, work, etc.

Here are five smart ways to practice social safety:

1. **Be picky.** Don't accept a friend request from someone you don't know. When following others on Twitter or Instagram, keep it to people who share your common interests and hopefully common friends. Be careful about sharing too much personal information.

2. **Be discreet.** When it comes to posting pictures for the whole world to see, remember, the whole world CAN see them. This means future employers and potential pervs. A good general rule is don't post anything that you wouldn't want your grandparents to see. Would grandma want to see you in a bikini making a duck face and sticking your ass out at passersby? I highly doubt it. So you probably don't want to post that one. Keep it clean.

3. **Ignore it.** If you begin receiving emails or private messages on Facebook, or Tweets from strangers who sound fishy, don't respond to them. We know sometimes it's tough not to reply to a nasty comment some stranger makes or even someone who appears sweet and is engaging you in conversation to extract more personal info from you. Delete, block and move on.

4. **#Latergram.** Never give people real time deets on your location. That also means no "checking in" when you're at the bar, club, or library. People shouldn't know where you are exactly when you're there. If you must post your location,

do it after you have left that place.

5. **Hide your home address.** If you own a website or blog, chances are your home address can easily be found online. When you buy a website domain name from a company like GoDaddy, you are required to register your home address, and this will be public information unless you pay an extra yearly fee to keep it private.

Let's Hear From You!
How do you practice social media safety?
#Hear Me Roar

Tweet Now:
Use #latergrams and never let the world
know where you are in real time.
#HearMeRoar

DATING DEFENSE

Chances are, this is one of the most exciting times of your life when it comes to dating. There's flirting, butterflies, and excitement. The more complicated stuff comes a little later on when you're ready to settle down. But for now, it's fun!

However, if you're not practicing dating defense, you could be putting yourself at risk.

Statistics say that approximately one in four college age women is date raped or experiences an attempted date rape during her college years.

AND

Eighty-four percent of women who have been date raped **knew** their attackers.

AND THIS

Approximately **ninety percent** of date rapes happen with **alcohol** involved.

AND WTF?

In one study, approximately thirty-three percent of men said that if they could escape date rape without detection, they would rape someone.

So yeah, the stats are frightening, and the thirty-three percent of guys polled in that survey definitely SUCK! So let's talk about ways that we can defend ourselves against these horrible statistics and still have a healthy and joyful dating life whether we're dating online or in person.

Online Dating:

Finding love online is now more popular and more accepted than ever. Lots of people have found love, a new friend, or sometimes just a hot date. Online dating can be fun as long as you wear your safety goggles!

The following are seven rules of dating defense when you meet someone online whether you've swiped away on Tinder or gone the more traditional route like eHarmony or Match.com.

1. Google His Ass!

Be a good spy girl. A potentially safe date's Google results will have things like his LinkedIn profile and Facebook page first, and/or his own personal or business website, not his criminal record. Be sure to check all of the results that come up and don't give up after the first few.

If he has a website, it's a no-brainer to check it out. Find out what he does for work if you don't already know, and make sure it matches what he's already told you. His LinkedIn profile, if you can get access to it, will show you a bit of his professional history and recommendations by others. Just remember that his professional life can be very different from his social life and that is why you'll need to dig a bit deeper.

If you can't see his Facebook profile without being his friend, see if you have any friends in common. If you do, it may not be a bad idea to reach out to them and find out a little more about your mystery date. Otherwise, there's no harm in friending him to get to see into his social world a bit more. Look out for warning signals like posts that degrade women, angry or depressed tirades, or organizations that he "likes" that also seem to set off warning alarms in your head.

Then check out any other social media profiles he may have like Twitter, Instagram, Vine, Youtube, etc. Scan through and look for similar warning signs. Also look for great signs like nice posts about his sisters or mom. And it goes without saying, you'll also get to see if he's truly single!

If he passes all of your online tests, be sure to have multiple phone conversations with him before you actually meet. We've heard of so many instances where girls will email with their suitors for weeks and arrange a date without ever picking up the phone. People can disguise themselves in email by scripting and re-writing their responses. But in a live phone chat, you will get to see his true colors a bit better.

2.   Get The Gang Involved

If you have a roommate or bestie, always be sure to keep her informed of where and when you are planning on meeting your dates. You should also check in with her at the end of your date when you've gotten home safely.

Other great ways of getting the gang in on it would be to suggest that your date meets your friends at some point in the date. Pick a bar or restaurant that is close to a location your friends are at on that particular day or night. For example, if all of your friends are at someone's house or dorm for dinner, suggest a fun "drop in" to meet the gang before you head out to dinner on your own. You can also do this at the end of your evening and time it so you can have your friends get you home safely.

Check out Kitestring. It's an app that makes sure you get home safely. You give it your emergency contacts and let it know when you are somewhere unsafe. It will text you later, and if you don't answer it will alert your loved ones that something may be wrong. It can't defend you against predators, but you'll never go missing without a trace.

3.   Arrange An Intermission

There are many ways to plan an intermission, or pause, during the date where you can check in with a friend.

Arrange a time toward the halfway point to excuse yourself to the bathroom and send your friend/roommate/sibling a text to check in. Or, you can have them set a reminder to call or text you at a certain time during the date.

If you haven't arranged an intermission with a friend in advance but your intuition is telling you that you should end this date, fake it. Fake an "emergency" text or call from your friend who is having an "emergency" that you will need to tend to immediately. Nothing too dramatic, you'll need to make it believable. Or simply tell your date you want to leave, period.

If you live in a city where you drive, it's much easier to get to your car and leave. If you are in a non-driving city, like New York, then you have to make sure he isn't going to walk you home. Send your check-in buddy a text to expect you home shortly and grab a cab.

4. Keep It Public At First

A daytime date in public is your safest bet. A coffee shop, café, or the on-campus hangout are public enough to have some good conversation and get to know someone. Go to brunch on the weekend and have plans to meet up with your friends when your date is done so your date doesn't have to walk you home and see where you live.

As your dates progress and things are looking good and your date wants to go out at night, suggest restaurants, wine bars, and pubs where you are a familiar face. Is there a bar where everybody knows your name? If so, take him there! Get him introduced to as many people as you know who work there or are regulars there. Here you should be testing his reaction to meeting new people to see whether he is relaxed about it or whether he doesn't seem to want to know anybody but you.

A guy who brags about his culinary talents and wants to cook dinner for you on the first few dates has major potential creep factor. Yes, it makes him sound sweet and nurturing and visions of the Naked Chef dance in your head, but remember at this point he is still basically a stranger.

Once you're in his place, you have entered his territory. This shouldn't happen until you are completely confident that he is a trustworthy guy and that you are ready to get a little physical. If you aren't ready, then do not go. Lots of guys read a yes to this kind of invitation as a yes to sex. I make her dinner, she gives me sex. And if you go and tell him you're not ready for all that and you only came for the prime rib, it may tick him off a bit. The best way to avoid that is to decline the invite and suggest a restaurant instead. Be honest with him. Tell him you're just not ready to go to his place yet, but you can't wait to taste his delightful cooking. He should completely understand that it is way too early to be going to his place for a romantic meal. If not, then maybe he should hit the road.

5. Group Date

Going out in groups is the safest way to get to know someone. This works well for people who have been set up on a blind date by mutual friends or coworkers. Bring him out to your friend's birthday party or to the weekend brunch that your friends religiously indulge in.

For the professional single woman, this could be a challenge to constantly have to rally her friends to go out so she doesn't have to be alone on a date. It's also tough to get to know someone when there are constantly other people around. However, with that said, it's a safer way to date, in the beginning stages anyway.

6. Stay Sober! Or Close To It.

Let's address the drinks, ladies. Have you ever woken up and not remembered how you got home the night before? We have! It's safe to say that it's a bad idea to get drunk on a date with someone you barely know.

First of all, your inhibitions are lowered which could lead

to making bad decisions, like going home with a guy on a first date. Second, our bodies mixed with alcohol are like one big chemical reaction that sometimes you cannot predict. So why risk it? Third, alcohol can act like a magnifier. So, if you're with a guy who may be a bit more aggressive than you'd like, chances are after a couple of drinks, he's going to be even more so. You're going to need your wits about you to stand your ground.

For your safety, follow these **Ten Cocktail Commandments**:

1. Don't drink on a first date, ever.

2. Stick to your limit, which should only be one or two drinks AFTER you have gotten to know your date. (Maybe a few weeks of dating.)

3. Never drink on an empty stomach.

4. Always watch when your drink is being prepared so nobody is able to slip anything into it.

5. Keep your drink in your sight at all times for the same reason as #4. Yes, that means taking it to the bathroom with you.

6. Sip slowly. Make it last as long as possible and drink one glass of water for every drink you have.

7. Never have a second drink within one hour of finishing your first.

8. Stay away from sugary mixers. They mess with your blood sugar big time, setting you up for a major crash.

9. No shots, ever!

10. Oh, and make sure you're twenty-one, it's the law.

Here are some things to keep in mind:

- When drinking dabbles in the danger zone is when you should rethink the drink. For example, if you're drinking to the point of blacking out then it's definitely time to cut way back.

- If you don't want to drink—great! Don't ever feel like you should.

- And if you want to drink—great! Just know your limits and practice safety.

- Real friends don't force you to do something you don't want to do NOR do they make you feel bad about not doing it. (Take us for example—Lindsey doesn't drink at all and Jenn enjoys a healthy glass of wine or two from time to time. Drinking or not drinking is totally cool either way. And it's a personal choice. Respect your friends.)

So you're out at a party and don't want to drink? Try our fun mocktail recipes on Page 120. You can have a fun drink to carry around with you all night without the side-effects to follow.

7. Say No to Preeps

Preep = potential creep

A preep is someone that your gut tells you NOT to go on a date with. You've read his text countless times and can't get that sentence out of your head because it sounded rude, obnoxious, overbearing, sexual, or too forward. Or, you've spoken on the phone and the hairs went up on the back of your neck over something he said. Whatever it is, something is telling you not to go out with him. Listen to your gut!

In the book Gift of Fear (which Oprah loves, need we say more?) Gavin De Becker explains how our intuition and feeling fear is our biggest gift. Often times, we are told by others not to listen to our guts, that we are being silly, paranoid, or have an overactive imagination. He writes:

"Can you imagine an animal reacting to the gift of fear the way some people do, with annoyance and disdain, instead of attention? No animal in the wild, suddenly overcome with fear, would spend any of its mental energy thinking, 'It's probably nothing.' Yet we chide ourselves for even momentarily giving validity to the feeling that somebody is behind us on a seemingly empty street, or that someone's unusual behavior might be sinister. Instead of being grateful to have a powerful internal resource, grateful for the self-care, instead of entertaining the possibility that our minds might actually be working for us and not just playing tricks on us, we rush to ridicule the impulse. We, in contrast to every other creature in nature choose not to explore—and even ignore—survival signals."

Listen to your intuition while dating, shopping, working out, at home, at work, inside, outside, and everywhere. If you feel fear, remember it's a gift. Time to rethink that date, walk to your car, route home, or whatever it is and abort mission.

Let's Hear From You!
When has your intuition saved your butt?
#HearMeRoar

Tweet Now:
Always listen to your intuition. If it feels off, it probably is.
#HearMeRoar

Six Questions to Ask Yourself Before You Go on a Date with a Stranger

1. **What is my date's full name?** You better know this! You're not just going out with HotGuy86 that you met online. And by now you have Googled his ass and verified key information on him.

2. **Who else knows where I'm going other than my date?** Be sure to tell your roommate, your sibling, or parent your full itinerary for the evening. Ask them to check in on you with a text once or twice throughout the evening at a specific time. This way you can check your phone at that specific time and not have to be fiddling with it all night taking time away from getting to know your Mr. Maybe.

3. **Where are we meeting?** He's not picking you up on your first date and taking you somewhere. Tell him you'll meet him at the chosen public location, preferably one that you are familiar with and maybe even friends with the barista, server, or bouncer.

4. **How am I getting home?** Be sure to have a plan to get yourself home safely or have someone you trust pick you up. Don't let a complete stranger know where you live on your first date unless you both live on campus, and then it's inevitable. Just don't let him in!

5. **Do I have enough cash on me in case I need to ditch the date and grab a cab?** Always carry enough cash with you in case of an emergency.

6. **Do I feel confident, strong, and comfortable setting my limits for the evening and communicating them when I need to?** If the answer is no, then do not go! There's no rush. There will be plenty of men around when you are ready and confident to set your limits.

Our friend, Alex Franzen is truly one of our self-confidence sheroes. The girl speaks and lives her truth and helps others do the same through writing and speaking.

Alex wrote several books, including an e-book called, How to Say No...Nicely.

Just for you, we had Alex wordsmith up some confident ways for YOU to say, "No," to a preep who asks you out. Here goes:

If the preep asks you out on a date, and he's sorta polite about it...

Say: No, thank you. My instincts are telling me we're not a match.

If the preep keeps pressuring you, or doesn't accept your answer...

Say: Actually, this isn't up for discussion. I said no.
[Ideally, you should leave the situation at this point. Don't give the preep a chance to keep pressuring you.]

If the preep says something gross or offensive like, "Your loss. I can tell that you need some good d*ck..."

Say: And THAT is exactly why I said no to begin with. Thanks for confirming that my instincts about you were correct.
[Then: remove yourself from the situation immediately! Walk away, hang up the phone, delete him from your social media friend-group, or whatever it takes.]

PS For more ways to say, "No," or for some other fun writing prompts, visit ***www.AlexandraFranzen.com***.

Let's Hear From You!
Who knows where you're going before you head out for a
night on the town?
#HearMeRoar

Tweet Now:
Saying no when you sense danger is a powerful tool.
#HearMeRoar

DATING, DOMESTIC VIOLENCE, AND D*CKS

Some guys are just creeps and once in a while you get caught up with a total dick. Trust us, we've been there. The sooner you can identify a creep and get him out of your life, the sooner you'll be able to move on to either work on yourself or open yourself up to a relationship that nurtures your growth and your soul.

Dating a creep can negatively affect your self-esteem and make you feel unworthy of real love. A creep can be emotionally abusive, manipulative, and downright mean. Sometimes this can turn into physical violence as well, but you may not see the signs right away.

Domestic violence is a serious issue and according to the National Coalition Against Domestic Violence, females between the ages of twenty and twenty-four years old are at the greatest risk of nonfatal intimate partner violence.

We define domestic violence as a pattern of abusive behavior in any relationship that is used by one partner to gain or maintain power and control over another intimate partner.

Here are twenty signs that you may be dating a creep: Does he…

1. Tease you excessively?

2. Make rude comments about you or other women in front of others?

3. Degrade women in general?

4. Tell misogynistic jokes?

5. Objectify women?

6. Try and control or manipulate you?

7. Keep you away from your friends?

8. Treat animals badly?

9. Get angry and/or violent when drinking alcohol or doing drugs?

10. Try to push you to go further than you're comfortable with sexually?

11. Yell at you?

12. Boss you around?

13. Pick fights with you?

14. Get extremely jealous?

15. Lie to you?

16. Cheat on you?

17. Not listen when you say no?

18. Tell you how to dress and act?

19. Say hurtful things and later on swear he never said those things?

20. Tire you out and make you doubt yourself? This usually comes in the form of a trivial argument that turns into a full-blown fight that lasts for hours and sometimes days.

These warning signs don't necessarily mean that a guy will turn to violence, but if he's not treating you well, it's time to ditch him anyway. Emotional abuse can sometimes be just as bad as physical abuse. It's also much easier to physically abuse a woman who is already being emotionally abused. Stand up for yourself from the beginning so you can avoid these situations altogether.

How To Get Out Of A Relationship With A Creep

While we understand that ending a relationship isn't always easy, using these prompts can help you get the process started. **If he's borderline rude and you want to end it before it gets worse...**

Say: I strongly believe that our relationship has run its course. We are not a match and I wish you the best.

If he's pressuring you or doesn't accept your answer...

Say: Actually, this isn't up for discussion. I said this relationship is over.
[Ideally, you should leave the situation at this point. Don't give the creep a chance to keep pressuring you.]

If the creep starts to get violent and threatens you...

Walk away, hang up the phone, and call in the big guns. Alert your friends, family, and the police immediately.

Once you have ended this relationship, do not continue conversations with your ex. No calls, no texts, and no meetings.

If you find yourself in this situation here is a resource for help: National Domestic Violence Hotline: 1-800-799-SAFE (7233)

It's way better for your self-esteem to be single than to be dating a creep. There are plenty of nice guys out there. Let the ones who are worthy of your time find you.

In the meantime, work on being your best self! Only when you truly love and respect yourself can you attract your perfect match.

——————————— SURVIVOR STORY ———————————

One night in December, many years ago, I spoke to my ex-boyfriend on the phone. He sounded weird, like how he used to sound when he was using. It made me very nervous.

He asked me to pick him up at a friend's house which, of course, I did immediately. I parked outside and waited in the car for what seemed like forever. When he finally came outside, I knew as soon as I saw his face. The man I loved…who had put me through hell and back…who promised me being clean was ALL he cared about, second to only me…

He was high again.

As I drove to my apartment, I felt completely numb. Every so often he would open his eyes and try to convince me he was fine, but we both knew better. When we arrived, he walked inside and instantly fell asleep on my bed.

It took me awhile to find the pills and when I did, I flushed them. I wanted them out of my house and I wanted him out of my house. I woke him up and told him I needed to take him home. Before leaving, however, he realized that I had found the pills and that I was probably hiding them, or even worse, that I had flushed them. This realization sparked the scariest moment of my life.

He tore my apartment apart. My entire apartment. He threw everything, from my books to my dresser to my bed. He was like a monster and I could hardly get out of his way.

"Where are they?!" he yelled, while smashing me up against the wall. "What the fuck did you do? Why did you go through my shit? You are such a bitch. I will fucking kill you!"

After struggling a bit, somehow I managed to escape his grip and I quickly left the apartment. With nowhere to go at 3 in the morning, I drove around aimlessly. Half an hour later I cautiously went back home, but the drugs had taken over; he was calm again. I counted my blessings, got him in the car, and rushed to take him to his house.

When I arrived back at my apartment, alone, I tended to the destruction. I wasn't exactly sure when my roommates would come back home, so even though I was exhausted, I cleaned up everything. I would need a new dresser, but it was still usable. My bookcase and bed were okay.

I wanted to be okay too…

When I was done cleaning, I called off work and let myself cry for hours. In four years I did all I could to make our relationship work. Somehow, I still failed. I wasn't enough for him to change. He wasn't enough for me to be happy.

Terrified and heartbroken, I decided to end the relationship. That night wasn't the first time he used physical aggression to control and manipulate me, but I knew it needed to be the last.

The light bulb finally came on and in that very moment my quest for self-love began. Five years later, I know that quest is far from over, as healing and self-love are a lifelong journey. It is the support of others, however, that reminds me that I'm worth taking the journey in the first place.

You are too.

-Akirah Robinson
www.akirahrobinson.com

Let's Hear From You!
What warning signs do you look for on a date?
#HearMeRoar

Tweet Now:
Emotional abuse is just as bad as physical abuse.
Get out as fast as you can.
#HearMeRoar

How To Make The Most Of Being Single

Times in your life when you are single can be spent wallowing in self-pity or completely rocking the world. It's your choice! Don't ever feel like you "need a guy" to feel worthy, whole, or complete. Use this time to explore sides of you that you never even knew existed.

Here are ten ways to rock out with your free time:

1. Be a brainiac. Choose a subject that's always interested you and become an expert. I want to expand my knowledge on _____(fill in the blank).

2. Learn to cook healthy meals for yourself.

3. Train for a physical challenge—for example, a triathlon, mud run, black belt, hike, etc.

4. Start a business!

5. Read self-help books. (We are both admitted self-help junkies and love it!)

6. Learn a foreign language.

7. Travel somewhere you've always dreamt about.

8. Make new girlfriends.

9. Write a blog.

And the best way you can spend free time to discover who you truly are is…

10. Contribute to society (locally or globally). This can be as easy as volunteering at the local soup kitchen or starting a toy drive for needy children. Getting outside of your own needs and focusing on giving to others who are less fortunate is one of the most liberating, humbling, and time worthy activities you can do.

Let's Hear From You!
How do you make the best of your single time?
#HearMeRoar

Tweet Now:
Contribute your gifts to the world!
#HearMeRoar

STREET SMARTS

Now that you've mastered the art of being social media safe, it's time to strengthen your street smarts.

What Are Street Smarts?

Having the experience and knowledge necessary to deal with the potential difficulties or dangers of life in any environment.

Why Are They Important?

1. So you can feel more confident while out and about.

2. To reduce your risk of danger.

3. To be able to fight back when you need to.

ABCs of SELF-DEFENSE

It's important to start with your ABCs:

Awareness

Boundaries

Communication

Awareness

Awareness is the very first step in self-defense. Being in a state of awareness can have many meanings. On the most superficial, it means being aware of your surroundings—knowing who and what is near or around you. On a deeper level, awareness can mean what's going on inside of you and how that is being projected outwardly. For example, your fear can be noticed from your posture.

Since we are talking about self-defense and reducing your chances of being in a risky situation, let's focus on our awareness of our surroundings.

Any time you are outside of a safe place, like your home, you should always be aware of your surroundings. Look around you and make mental notes. Look at the buildings, the space between buildings, the wide open spaces, and the spaces there could potentially be someone hiding. When indoors, always know where the exits are and how you would get to one safely if there was an emergency inside.

Next, check out the people (and even animals) that you are sharing the space with. While walking home at night, look at the other people on the street. No need to stare; just glance, make eye contact, and keep moving. By doing this, you've removed the element of surprise. No longer can someone sneak up on you and catch you off guard. You've seen them and they know it!

We tend to put up many obstacles to ourselves being fully aware. Check the list below to see how your behavior is hindering your awareness.

Do you do any of the following?

- Talk on your phone while walking outdoors?
- Text while walking outdoors?
- Walk or jog outdoors with your headphones on listening to music?
- Wear sunglasses that block your peripheral vision?
- Blast the radio in your car while driving with your doors unlocked?
- Bury your head in a book on a bus, train, or subway?

If you've answered yes to any of these questions, you have been practicing being unaware. But that's ok because now you're aware of it! Make some simple changes and build a habit of being attentive with your sight, sound, touch, and intuition. Here's a few ways to do just that:

1. **Observe:** While commuting to class or work, start noticing other people's awareness practices. Observe how easy it would be to surprise someone who is not paying attention to their surroundings. Then choose not to be like them.

2. **Listen:** Practice listening to the sounds around you as well as other people's words. Not only will it help you pick up clues more easily, but it will also make you a more effective communicator.

3. **Meditate:** Sitting still and being quiet helps hone your sixth sense, or the power of your unconscious. The sixth sense is connected to your intuition and will help you sense danger so you can act before it's too late.

Street Smart Awareness

Keys are in your hand, you're ready to leave your home, dorm, or apartment to head on your date, your party, or out for your run. Here are five questions to ask yourself before you leave the house:

1. If I'm driving: do I have enough gas to get there and home and then some?

2. If I'm walking: what's the most direct, well-lit route I can take?

3. If I'm taking public transportation, what are the safest and most direct routes I can take without having to transfer too many times and which will get me the closest to my destination?

4.   Who else knows where I'm going and who I'm going to be with?

5.   What improvised weapon am I carrying on my body?

Boundaries

Setting physical boundaries is crucial to protecting your body from a potential predator. We all have different comfort levels when it comes to our space. For example, some people like to hug and others can't stand it. But, when it comes to strangers, you definitely need to know your boundaries.

On the street, keep aware of people around you and how close they need to be to you. On a crowded street or subway during rush hour, it may be completely normal and necessary to be close to someone. However, at 10 p.m. walking down a deserted street there should be nobody even close to your personal space.

Find Your Personal Space

Stand up and spread both of your arms out to the side as far as they'll go. Now turn until you make a complete circle. That imaginary line that you just drew with your hands is going to symbolize the boundary of your personal space. Nobody should invade your personal space unless you have invited them into it.

If someone has invaded your personal space you have two options:

1.   Physically move away from that person so you can re-establish your personal space.

2.   Confront the person who has invaded your space. Tell them to get away from you. Or you may have to be more forceful with your language and/or your body and remove them from your space.

Communication

> "I speak two languages, Body and English."
> - Mae West

How we communicate is monumentally important in street smarts. Body language is the most important factor in choosing to be a target or not. We've read that physiology is more important than tonality and vocabulary when communicating. So how you deliver your message with your body and tone is more important than what you actually say when reclaiming your space, privacy, or fighting back against a potential attacker.

Predators look for weak and vulnerable targets. Clues of vulnerability are:

- slouched shoulders
- head down
- toes pointing in
- distracted targets (i.e. on their phone, headphones in ears, looking frazzled, searching through their purse, etc.)

In order for you to communicate effectively with your body, we came up with these BODY TALK guidelines:

B – Be Alert: If you're too sleepy, light-headed, or drunk, you should not be alone outside. After giving blood at the doctor's office, you may feel woozy. Or maybe you're coming down with a cold and feel dizzy. Then there's the possibility that you drank too much darn booze and all of a sudden need to leave the bar where you and your friends are. In any situation, always make sure you have trusted friends with you to get you home safely. If you cannot be both physically and mentally alert, you should not be outside.

O – Off your phone: Being on your phone is the worst distraction when you are out on the town by yourself. Talking or texting on the phone makes you a walking target to a predator. He sees that you're distracted, and it gives him a perfect opportunity to surprise you. Remember from Jenn's intro—this happened to her. It doesn't matter who's on the other line. That person won't be able to protect you in the moment. Keep your cell phone in your purse and pay attention to your surroundings.

D – Dress responsibly: Don't shoot the messenger here, ladies. We love dressing sexy for girls' night out or sexy date night, but if we're heading out on the town with our boobs hanging out and a dress up to our butt cheeks, we know that we might attract some negative attention.

Y – Yell with your entire body and voice when you are threatened and want to attract attention. That means scream from your belly, not your throat, throw your hands in the air, run, and do whatever you can to get others to hear you.

T – Tall spine: Keep your head up and shoulders back. Your posture is a way your body communicates to a predator, consciously or unconsciously. When a predator sees a woman looking down with her shoulders slumped, he sees weakness and vulnerability. Walking tall, even if you're short, gives off a sense of confidence and self-assurance. Walk as if you could kick butt in any situation even if you may be scared. Fake it 'til you make it!

A – Alarm in hand: Have your personal alarm ready to sound off in case of danger. A personal alarm is a device that you can attach to your keychain, and when you pull the pin, an alarm will sound and be heard up to three hundred feet away. The sound will hopefully deter an attacker from proceeding because he doesn't want to get caught. We recommend Sabre's personal alarm. (See Resources)

L – Look at everyone in your path: Making eye contact with everyone in your path may feel funny at first, but you'll get used to it. It's a great safety tip for many reasons. First, anyone that you come in contact with knows that you have seen him or her. Meaning, they can no longer sneak up on you and surprise you. You're also scanning who's around you and checking out their body language. You may find that someone has been staring at you and possibly following you. Lastly, by checking everyone out you'll have a better chance of identifying someone if an attack on you or someone else were to occur.

K – Keys out: Carry your keys in your hand, not in your purse, for two reasons. First, if you are being followed to your home or car, you can quickly key in, get safely inside, and lock the doors behind you without fumbling around your purse for your keys. Second, your keys could be used as a weapon.

Let's Hear From You!
What new habits will you develop
to help you communicate confidence?
#HearMeRoar

Tweet Now:
Awareness, boundaries, and communication are
the ABCs of self-defense.
#HearMeRoar

VERBAL KUNG FU

Verbal Kung Fu is essentially fighting without fighting. More simply, how to use one's words to prevent, de-escalate, or end an attempted verbal assault.

How To Defend Against A Verbal Attack

Verbal attacks come in all sizes and severities. Whether it's the bully at school or work insulting you or a stranger on the street threatening you. Sometimes our egos get the best of us and we want to confront that person head on, or we get too intimidated to say anything at all.

Ideally, we need to defend ourselves without escalating the situation into a full blown screaming match or violent episode. There are full books dedicated to this subject alone, so we are just going to give you some quick tips for defending yourself against verbal attacks.

If you feel offended by someone's comment and this person is a family member, a date, a classmate, or a workplace peer, chances are you'll probably have to deal with that person on an ongoing basis. Here are some tips on how to deal:

1. **Breathe.** Take five if you need it, even if that person is standing right in front of you.

2. **Check your posture.** Stand confidently with your head up and shoulders back before you express yourself verbally. Make eye contact with that person.

3. **Clarify and ask questions.** Sometimes someone may sound like they are trying to offend you, but they aren't meaning to at all. Or sometimes people who suck may be giving you a backhanded insult that you can bring to the forefront. You can say something like, "I just heard you say _____,

am I correct in thinking you meant _____?"

4. **Set limits.** If the person who is offending you keeps going, keeps trying to manipulate or insult you, be the bigger and more mature person and set your limits. You can say something like, "It was nice talking to you, I'm late for another meeting," or, "Wow, I'm sorry that you feel that way. Gotta go now," or, "I love that we can disagree on this subject. Isn't that great?!"

5. **End the conversation.** You can do this by saying goodbye, thanking them for their opinion, or physically removing yourself from the person or group.

Dealing with strangers while outside of a safe environment could be more intense and involve more risk. Obviously, there are so many different scenarios we could list here, but we are only going to cover a few.

The following are examples of gross situations where you may have to exert your power just enough so the jerk on the other end knows you mean business.

Jerk: **You're looking kind of chubby these days.**
You: *Thanks, I like my curves.*

Jerk: **Whistling**
You: *Keep walking*

Jerk: **Smile. (And when you don't…) Ok, be a bitch then.**
You: *Ignore. Make a weird face instead.*

Jerk: **Hey baby, how you doing?**
You: *Great, when I'm left alone.*

Jerk: **Hey baby, nice ass!**
You: *It is, too bad you'll never get a piece.*
         (OR just ignore and walk away.)

Jerk: You're just not my type. I like girls with bigger _____
(tits, ass, etc.)

You: Perfect, because I like guys with bigger brains.

Jerk: (Getting close to your personal space and your
intuition flags are up) Hey, you have a minute? Are
you in a rush to get somewhere? Can you help me
with _____? Let me help you with your bags.

*You: No! Get out of my space. Get away from me. Yes, I'm in a
rush. (Keep power walking. Run. All depending on the
situation, but be fierce!)*

Let's Hear From You!
Is there a situation you are in where verbal
kung fu may work well?
#HearMeRoar

Tweet Now:
Use verbal kung fu to de-escalate or
end a verbal assault.
#HearMeRoar

THE 3 Fs: FIT, FIERCE, AND FEMININE

Be Fit

Being fit is not just about looking good. Being fit can help you defend your body against harm internally, emotionally, and physically.

Internally:

When your body is fit it's able to fight off invaders like bacteria and viruses so you don't get sick as often. Exercise helps boost your immune system, and sweating helps release toxins from your body.

Emotionally:

A strong body and strong mind go together. When you are physically fit, you feel better mentally. Exercise releases endorphins, or happy chemicals, that make us feel good. When we feel good, we have a better outlook on life and feel less stressed. When we feel less stressed, we can tackle everyday problems with ease. And when life throws us curveballs, we are that much more prepared to deal with them mentally when we have a strong body and a regular exercise routine.

Physically:

Being fit increases your chances of survival. You need to be able to run from any sort of danger, and a strong body can help you fight when you need to.

Fitness does not have to be complicated. To design a balanced exercise program, it has to include three areas of fitness: cardio, strength and flexibility.

Cardiovascular fitness entails getting your heart rate up and sustaining it for at least thirty minutes per session. This can be anything from a brisk walk to work to a bicycle ride around campus. Choose what you enjoy doing like jogging, biking, swimming, kickboxing, or dancing. Include this into your lifestyle at least three to four times per week to feel fantastic.

Strength training is important for strong muscles. But you don't have to be a bodybuilder to get the benefits of strength training. You can follow a workout video, hit the gym, or do bodyweight exercises in your room for just twenty minutes twice a week. Three simple exercises you can do anywhere are squats for your butt and legs, push-ups for shoulders, arms, and chest and plank for a strong core.

The last part of any good fitness routine, and most overlooked, is flexibility. Stretch, do yoga, or use a foam roller to release tension and tight muscles in order to defend against injury over time.

Try this exercise on days when you're just not feeling it:

Exercise makes me feel _____, _____ and _____.

I know that exercise is good for my body and my mind.

As soon as my session of _____ is complete I will feel _____. That feeling alone is enough to get me moving and sweating.

Six Tips for the Outdoor Fitness Buff

Always remember to be safe while you're getting your sweat on whether indoors or outdoors. For all of you outdoor fitness buffs, this is for you:

1. **Light up:** If you can't fit your run/walk/hike in your schedule until sundown, be sure to carry a small flashlight so you can always check out your surroundings. You can also wear a headlamp or use a flashlight app on your smartphone.

2. **Reflect:** It's equally important that drivers and cyclists can see you, as it is that you see them. Buy some cool reflective gear. There are vests, armbands, and blinking lights that are easy to attach to your body or clothes.

3. **Check your feet:** You may love running barefoot, but will you be able to take off in a full sprint if someone was chasing you? If you're a barefoot sport shoe wearer, stick to using them during daylight and wear your sneakers at night.

4. **Get spicy:** Contrary to popular belief, pepper spray is legal to carry in all fifty states. You can attach one to your keychain or buy runner's pepper spray and carry it with you while out and about. If attacked you can spray it in your attacker's face making it very difficult for him to catch you as you sprint away to safety.

5. **Sound the alarm:** If pepper spray isn't for you, as mentioned earlier a personal alarm is a great alternative. This will only work if the threat of being caught scares off your attacker. This is why we always suggest self-defense training for times when you are left with no other options.

6. **Listen up:** We know music is one of the best motivators when it comes to an intense bout of cardio, but it also drowns out one of your most important senses for sniffing out danger. When your music is blasting, you can't hear a potential threat if he sneaks up right behind you (we know because it's happened to Jenn while she was listening to a voicemail on her cellphone). Leave your music at home if you're exercising outdoors.

Let's Hear From You!
What's your favorite part of fitness?
What areas can you improve on?
#HearMeRoar

Tweet Now:
Being fit isn't just about looking good.
Being fit increases your chances of survival.
#HearMeRoar

Be Fierce

Your body is important when defending against danger, but your attitude is the most important weapon you have. It may just need a little training.

Think of the animal kingdom. Even the most timid and gentle female animals will lash out if they think they, or their babies, are under attack.

So maybe we're not wild animals, but we believe all women have an inner strength that we can tap into when we need it most. We like to call it your inner She Beast. Chances are you have witnessed this She Beast at least once in your life. Perhaps you were defending yourself against someone or something that was taking advantage of you? Or maybe you used it on someone who was taking advantage of someone else?

Sometimes we need this power to get us through an emotional heartbreak or to overcome a tragic event that happened in our lives. Whatever it is, remember that you have this power simply by believing that you do because you are a woman. Then, it's like a muscle—the more you use it the stronger it will become.

Perhaps there was a time in your life where you were taken advantage of by someone who sucks. A powerful exercise could be any time that you start to replay that scene in your head, flip the script. Visualize yourself being the victor of the situation and coming out of it unharmed and at peace.

How do we tap into our She Beast power?

- By doing things outside of our comfort zone (i.e. public speaking, jumping out of a plane, applying for a big scholarship, program, or job)

- Remembering times that we used our inner She Beast power

- Visualizing ourselves flipping the script

────────── SHE BEAST SURVIVOR STORY ──────────

I was fifteen years old when I was attacked while walking home one night. That night, like many others, I walked with a friend until the last two blocks where we went our separate ways. About one hundred yards from entering my parents' house, a man jumped out of an alleyway and attacked me. Until this day, I have no idea what he held in his hand. I knew the object was black and solid as he cracked me across the left cheek with it. He leaped at me and tried pulling my windbreaker over my head so I couldn't see anything as he tried to throw me to the ground.

Survival instinct kicked in as my adrenaline rushed. I have always been a runner and my legs are the strongest part of my body. I fought with him as he tried pushing me to the ground, and my legs wouldn't give in. I screamed a sound of complete terror. I didn't know a noise like that could come from me. Because I kept fighting and screaming, my attacker eventually ran away and was never caught. Through my police descriptions, they were able to determine that my attacker was at the local teen hangout and watched me all night and eventually followed me home.

Physically, my face was bruised from where he hit me, and my body was sore the next day. But, the majority of my injuries were mental and emotional. I could have been beaten, raped, kidnapped, and even killed. I have no idea what he had planned. I'm thirty-four years old and still remember that night like it was yesterday. I still walk down the street holding my keys as a weapon or carry pepper spray in my purse. My heart still pounds uncontrollably when I'm walking down a dark street at night. I'm missing a sense of safety and security that is due every woman.

When I tell this story to others, through no fault of their own, they sometimes don't understand the impact it's had on me (or other victims). They often sympathize and say, "I'm sorry that happened to you." But until it happens to you or someone you love, it's hard to grasp the impact such an event has. It goes with you everywhere.

- Sheila B.

Let's Hear From You!
Have you ever released your inner She Beast?
How did it feel?
#HearMeRoar

Tweet Now:
Be fierce. Release your inner She Beast.
#HearMeRoar

Be Feminine

Guess what? Being feminine is an asset, not a liability. Regardless of anything you have ever been led to believe about women being the weaker gender, let us remind you, it is women who have typically given birth, raised families, and complained a lot less when we got sick.

Women have been discriminated against and abused throughout history and are the victims of nine out of ten sexual assaults that occur. Yet, we still prevail.

Let's use our femininity in our favor.

Know Your Weapons

Your body can turn into a weapon if you need to defend it.

Your head can head-butt.

Your mouth can scream really loudly!

Your teeth can bite.

Your elbows can strike.

Your fists can punch.

Your fingers can gouge.

Your knees can strike.

Your feet can kick.

Did you realize how dangerous you could be? Even everyday items that we have on our bodies can turn into weapons.

Your purse can swing.

Your cell phone can strike.

Your (metal) water bottle can hit.

Your pen can stab.

Your keys can jab.

Your rolled up magazine edges can slice.

Your stiletto heels can pierce.

I bet you won't look at those items the same anymore. Two items we recommend carrying with you:

A Sabre Personal Alarm—this will hopefully deter your attacker in fear that he may get caught.

Sabre Pepper Spray—sometimes, an attacker won't care about the noise. Perhaps he's on drugs or has a mental disorder. In this case, the second item we recommend carrying is a Sabre pepper spray. When sprayed in your attacker's face, it will burn his skin and eyes and hopefully disrupt his vision, allowing you to run to safety.

Know Your Targets

Sometimes, the unthinkable happens and you may have to fight for your life. Now is when you need to think like the tiger in the wild and become the attacker. You will need to fight until you can escape to safety.

There are many effective targets on the human body. However, unless you are training in self-defense, learning pressure points and how to strike effectively, you may have a hard time making any impact on your attacker.

The following three targets are easy to find, easy to hit, and will have the most impact on your attacker. At the very least, your attacker should be distracted long enough for you to get out of a hold and run for safety.

Eyes

The eyeballs are great targets for a few reasons. If you poke someone in the eye, his automatic reaction is to turn his head upwards. This then opens up another great target—the throat. Next, if you scratch someone's eyes out he'll have a hard time seeing you run in the opposite direction. And let's not forget the pain that someone will experience when getting their eyeballs jabbed with your fingers, thumb, or keys. The pain will be unbelievable, and if he does have you in a hold, chances are he is letting go and flailing which gives you the opportunity to escape.

Throat

The throat or neck is another effective target because if you hit it straight on with a tight fist, at the windpipe or trachea, you will disrupt your attacker's breathing at the very least. While he starts coughing, you may be able to get away. The carotid artery runs up and down the sides of the throat. If you were to hit someone on the side of the throat you can disrupt oxygen flow to the brain. If done correctly, your attacker may be on the floor or unconscious.

Groin

You probably learned this one on the playground when some boy got hurt when a ball or a foot hit him in the groin. He doubled over and probably shed some tears. It hurts, especially if you strike it correctly.

Knee a guy in the groin for most impact in an upward direction, so you get him in the balls. You can also punch or even grab with a tight grip and squeeze.

These are great starting tips for self-defense, and we highly recommend that you invest your time into training in a self-defense class and practicing with the *Stilettos and Self Defense* DVD series.

—————————— SURVIVOR STORY ——————————

"I was leaving the library one day, and when I got to my car, a creepy looking man came out of nowhere. He demanded that I give him my purse. I threw my purse in his face and kicked him as hard as I could right in his nuts! He went down and started to puke. I could still hear him puking when I ran away. It was all very shocking."

– Maria B.

Let's Hear From You!
Do you have the tools to defend yourself?
#HearMeRoar

Tweet Now:
My body is a weapon.
#HearMeRoar

SECTION 3
FOOD & HEALTH

"One cannot think well,
love well, sleep well,
if one has not
dined well."

– Virginia Woolf

Defending your health from people who suck is just as important as defending your emotions and body! And let's face it—when we eat healthy, we can think clearer and have the physical strength and energy to kick ass in all areas of life!

So MANY people come to us and say things like, "I don't have time to eat healthy." Or, "Eating healthy is so hard!" We say, "Do you have time to feel like garbage all day?"

When it comes to your health, there's no room for excuses. Kick-ass people don't make excuses. They do their research (like you're doing here) and take on challenges in order to become their best self.

FIERCE FOOD GUIDELINES

We are bombarded by the media about the latest trendy diets and celebrity weight loss stories. The media tends to WAY overcomplicate food. And the food industry doesn't help either. Low fat, sugar-free, high protein are a few of the claims that marketers will use on packages to disguise processed foods as health foods. Of course, this can be ultra-confusing!

What we need to do is tune out the noise and listen to our real needs. Let's get back to the basics. Here are our simple, yet effective Fierce Food Guidelines:

Read Your Labels

Smart chicks read labels. Here are your label rules of thumb:

1. If you can't pronounce it, don't eat it.
2. If it sounds like a chemical, it probably is! Stay clear.
3. If sugar is a top ingredient, reconsider.
4. If the ingredient list is longer than 5, don't buy it.
5. If it has artificial sweeteners, forget it.

And to quote Michael Pollan, "If it's a plant, eat it. If it's made in a plant, don't."

These guidelines aren't complicated. They are easy, effective and can help clean up even the grossest diet we've ever seen.

Eat Color

Simple yet, profound. Colors of the rainbow on your plate can boost your mood and your energy. Each color provides specific vitamins and minerals your body needs. Go ahead and pile the following foods on your plate.

Veggies like: Broccoli, bok choy, carrots, cauliflower, cucumber, collard greens, eggplant, kale, lettuce, peppers, spinach, squash, tomatoes and zucchini

Fruit like: Apples, bananas, blueberries, cantaloupe, grapes, honeydew, peaches, pineapple, plums, nectarines, raspberries, strawberries and watermelon

Eat Real Food

Eating real food. Simple enough, right? Real food is food that grows from the Earth and most likely will go bad if not eaten right away. This means fruits, vegetables, legumes, nuts and seeds, wild fish, and other animals that are raised as organically as possible on their natural diet and treated humanely.

If we all stuck to eating real food instead of processed foods there would be way less gross diseases out there.

So, keep it real, people.

Choosing Organic

So we'll let you in on a little secret! Choosing organic IS the way to go to ensure high quality freshness, the most nutrient content, and the least amount of pesticides. However, we also know that it is unrealistic for some people to eat organic ALL the time. So the following are two great cheat sheets from the Environmental Working Group.

In addition to The Dirty Dozen, we also recommend that if you eat animal based foods (eggs, dairy and meat) to try and buy them organic when possible.

The Dirty Dozen (always buy organic):

1. Peaches
2. Apples
3. Sweet Bell Peppers

4. Celery
5. Nectarines
6. Strawberries
7. Cherries
8. Pears
9. Grapes (Imported)
10. Spinach
11. Lettuce
12. Potatoes

The Clean Fifteen (no need to buy organic):

1. Avocadoes
2. Sweet corn
3. Pineapple
4. Cabbage
5. Sweet peas (frozen)
6. Onions
7. Asparagus
8. Mangoes
9. Papayas
10. Kiwis
11. Eggplant
12. Grapefruit
13. Cantaloupe
14. Cauliflower
15. Sweet potatoes

Drink Water

H20 does the body good—in more ways than one! Here are just some of the amazing benefits of water:

- Makes you feel fuller, faster
- Clears up your skin
- Promotes healthy digestion
- Reduces sugar cravings
- Removes toxins from your body
- Hydrates your muscles so you can exercise longer

Here are some smart ways to incorporate more water into your lifestyle:

- Invest in a nice BPA-free water bottle to use through-out the day. This will help you refill and drink up! (BPA is a chemical that sucks found in most plastic containers.)
- Add fresh fruit or vegetables for an added twang.

Our Favorite Fruit & Veggie Waters!

Strawberry Basil

Cucumber Mint

Lemon Lavender

Watermelon Mint

FIERCE FOODS

Now that we got the sucky foods out of the way, let's move on to the ass-kicking She-Beast foods that make you feel grounded, energized, focused and strong!

After all, you receive your energy from the food you eat. So if you eat a diet filled with highly processed foods, chances are you will feel a bit processed—unfocused and lousy.

However, a diet high in whole foods, will help you kick ass in all areas.

Below is a chart of some of the BEST foods for whatever scenario you are in!

How do you want to feel?	Foods to eat:
Grounded	Root vegetables like carrots, sweet potatoes, beets and turnips.
Energized	Leafy green vegetables like kale and spinach. Also green tea, raw cacao powder and bananas.
Focused	Foods that contain omega 3 fatty acids like wild salmon, seaweed, pumpkin seeds and walnuts.
Kick-Ass (A mix between high energy and strong!)	Leafy green vegetables like kale and spinach, bee pollen, black beans, chia seeds
Strong	Lean protein like eggs, fish, organic chicken, and grass fed beef
Sexy	Maca Powder, avocados, coconut oil, and oysters
Calm	Chamomile tea, almonds, berries, and dark chocolate

Let's Hear From You!
What's your favorite Fierce Food?
#HearMeRoar

Tweet Now:
I choose to nourish my body with fierce foods.
#HearMeRoar

The World's Easiest & Healthiest Snack List Ever

Sweet Snacks	Dark chocolate, carrots, blueberries, dates, grapes, strawberries, dried fruit
Savory Snacks	Nut crackers, rice crackers, corn tortilla chips, popcorn, salsa, kale chips, stuffed grape leaves, sardines, sauerkraut
Creamy Snacks	Hummus, guacamole, peanut butter, almond butter, sunflower butter, Greek yogurt, smoothies
Energizing Snacks	Carrots and hummus, edamame, trail mix, granola, apples with almond butter, banana with peanut butter

FOODS THAT SUCK

Just like people in your life that suck your energy or hurt you in some way, these foods act the same way. Aim to recognize where they hide on your plate and give 'em the boot!

Sugar

We are taking sugar on! What used to be a mere condiment is now a normal ingredient in almost every product on the shelf—from the usual cookies and cakes to even yogurt, bread, pasta sauce, and fruit mixes. This sneaky substance gets into everything, and guess what? It's not only just as addictive as cocaine, but it is also as energy sucking.

Sugar is the biggest culprit when it comes to unhealthy weight gain and obesity. It contributes to Type 2 Diabetes, blood sugar swings, mood swings, adrenal fatigue, and even cancers and heart disease.

Don't be sugar's bitch anymore. Take back your power (and your energy!).

Here are some safe tips to help you beat sugar for good:

Check Your Sugar

Sugar is the only ingredient that isn't required to show the "daily value percentage." And you know why? Because the food industry doesn't want you to know! Most likely because if you see, "500%" OVER your daily allotted intake, you probably wouldn't buy it. Then you wouldn't get addicted. Then the company wouldn't have repeat customers. And no money would be made from you! Seriously? The food industry sounds like a major preep to us. Stay clear and watch your numbers.

The average American consumes nineteen teaspoons of sugar in a day! Yikes, no wonder we are in so much trouble. Keep your daily sugar intake to under four teaspoons per day.

4g of sugar = 1 teaspoon
8g of sugar = 2 teaspoons
16g of sugar = 4 teaspoons

Always read the grams per serving for sugar and do your math. How many teaspoons of sugar are you consuming per day?

Know the Many Names of Sugar

This sneaky substance hides in almost everything and can be disguised as different names. Don't let these names fool you! Here are just a few of the many to steer clear of:

Brown sugar
Confectioner's sugar
Powdered Sugar
Corn Syrup
High Fructose Corn Syrup
Dextrose
Glucose
Honey
Invert Sugar
Lactose
Fructose
Levulose
Raw sugar

Sorbitol

Mannitol

Mallitol

Xylitol

Sucrose

How to cut down on sugar for good

- Stay hydrated. Drink plenty of water throughout the day. Sometimes dehydration can cause sugar cravings.

- Go for fruit first.

- Eat more protein throughout the day.

- Read your labels. If sugar is in the first three ingredients—stay clear!

- Never buy a food that has over 8g of sugar per serving. That's two teaspoons of sugar!

- Call a friend (sometimes we need our sweetness and nourishment from life—not food!)

Gluten

Gluten is a protein found in wheat, rye, barley, and malt. Many times, diets high in gluten can cause mood swings, brain fog, or stomach pains. Not everyone needs to go gluten free, but cutting back on foods made with non-organic wheat is probably a good idea.

Here are some great alternatives to try:

Quinoa

Brown Rice Pasta

Quinoa Pasta

Rice Crackers

Millet

Muesli

Gluten-free oats

Corn pasta

Rice (brown, black, wild)

Soba noodles (buckwheat)

Buckwheat Pancakes

Corn Tortillas

Processed Foods

Processed food just plain sucks. These foods are typically wrapped in bright color packaging and made in a lab. They usually contain some or most of the following: chemicals, additives, fillers, sugars, GMO's (genetically modified foods), trans fats and empty calories.

Stay away from the Five Worst Food Predators found in processed foods:

High fructose corn syrup (HFCS): This is the cheapest crap the food industry could create to sweeten foods and make them addictive. It's the number one source of calories in America, making us obese. This ingredient is a red flashing light NOT to buy or eat this food.

Monosodium glutamate (MSG): Used as a flavor enhancer, MSG is a shitty additive that when consumed in excess can lead to fatigue, depression, and headaches. Check in with your favorite take-out restaurant and frozen meals and make sure there's no MSG.

Food Dyes: These fake colorings like the yellow in your mac n' cheese or the red and blue found in candy and your favorite cereal are just plain gross! They are marketing tricks to make food look better and more appetizing. However, they are banned in many other countries and have been linked to ADHD and lower brain function. Um, NO THANKS!

Hydrogenated oils: These are basically fake fats that some creep made up in a lab and are now hidden in tons of baked goods and the crappy kinds of peanut butter. Before you buy those cookies, cakes, pretzels, breads, crackers and peanut butter, check the ingredient list for hydrogenated or partially hydrogenated oils. AKA TRANS FATS!

Artificial sweeteners: Just because a food is labeled "sugar-free" does not mean it is healthy. In fact, artificial sweeteners like Splenda®, Equal®, Nutrasweet®, and Sweet'N Low® are major preeps and should never be consumed. You may think you are quenching your sweet tooth but your brain knows better. Studies have shown that many people who drink diet soda actually gain weight because they eat more sugary foods throughout the day. Then there's the whole possible links to cancer thing. We say, screw the chemicals and stick to the pure stuff instead.

Keep the bees in business and use a touch of raw honey or pure maple syrup when you want a little sweet in your food.

And as for Stevia? We still prefer what nature provides, but this is another alternative that is better than the artificial stuff.

Let's Hear From You!
What food predators are you ready to kick to the curb?
#HearMeRoar

Tweet Now:
I'm cutting back on foods that suck:
sugar & processed foods.
#HearMeRoar

BEYOND FOOD

Ditch the Guilt—Practice Food Gratitude

I know we got the guidelines out of the way, but we want to encourage you to use them as mere guidelines and NOT restrictions. Because at the end of the day—real food IS meant to be pleasurable and enjoyable.

Are we saying to eat an entire carton of cookies in one sitting? No. But, if you want a treat at a party or after dinner, eat it and feel really damn good about it. Feeling any sense of guilt around food is robbing your body of joy, and it wreaks havoc on your body, causing you to experience digestive issues and unneeded stress and anxiety.

So if you cut yourself some slack and practice food gratitude—you can enjoy your treat without the guilt. Here are some ways:

- Think of food as an experience. Savor the experience. Take in all the senses. Smell your food, chew it slowly, and embrace the textures and tastes.

- Want to indulge in grandma's chocolate cake? Great! But first, think about the deep gratitude you have for the cake. Think about all the love and joy your grandma put into making it. Think about how it was truly made with love. Think about the pure joy you are feeling to experience this cake with your grandma. Feel extremely grateful.

- Give thanks. From kale to chocolate and from cupcakes to carrots—love and appreciate your food. Simply give thanks before each meal, snack, or treat. Just say a little, "Thank you for providing me with this great meal or snack." Remember, having access to food IS something to be grateful for.

Let's Hear From You!
What do you most appreciate about food?
#HearMeRoar

Tweet Now:
From kale to cupcakes, choose to eat with love.
#HearMeRoar

Ditch the Diet

Let's get straight with you—diets don't work. Yes, we know. We often wish for the miracle pill or magic diet to save the day.

However, confident girls ditch the diets and focus on feeling good in their bodies and skin!

Here are some fun ways to ditch the diet for good:

- Focus on how you feel mentally and physically.

- Have a fitness routine you love.

- Get rid of processed foods.

- Focus on eating more real food.

- Allow yourself healthy indulgences with no guilt attached.

Hone In & Get To Know Your Body

Let's get the facts straight—every BODY is literally different. That's why you and your girlfriend can go on the same diet. In a week, she loses ten pounds and you gain ten. It's because what works for one person, doesn't necessarily work for the next.

So rather than focusing on diets, deprivation, restriction and comparison, get really in tune with YOUR body. Treat it like a test lab. Figure out what your body really needs.

Do this by digging deeper. When you eat something, ask yourself how you feel—an hour later, two hours later, or the next day? Make mental or physical notes of the clues your body is telling you.

Use the chart below to get to know your body even more:

Food You Ate?	How You Feel 1 Hour Later	2 Hours Later?	The Next Day
Ex: Pizza	Bloated	Full	Tired

Let's Hear From You!
Are you getting to know your body
more through this exercise? Tell us your successes!
#HearMeRoar

Tweet Now:
Every BODY is different. Get to know your own!
#HearMeRoar

FIERCE FOOD RECIPES

We included some of our favorite recipes at the end of this book for you to enjoy! They are all really simple, easy, and whole-foods based.

We broke them down into four sections:

Mocktails (Start on page 120): Who said you needed alcohol to have fun? These are tasty and refreshing drinks that give you a natural buzz! (And you'll feel great the next day, too!)

Smoothies (Start on page 123): These smoothies are perfect for a nourishing breakfast, a mid-day snack, or even a quick and on-the-go lunch! Feel free to experiment with your own smoothies.

Filling Snacks (Start on Page 126): These simple snacks are meant to satisfy your craving and your hunger level. Great for in-between classes or on-the-go.

No Bake Treats (Start on page 132): If you are craving a sweet or savory treat, these no bake options are perfect for dorm living or if you just don't feel like baking!

Here's to kickin ass in the kitchen!

ODE TO PEOPLE (OR THINGS) THAT SUCK

By now you know that a fast food burger can drain the life out of you just like a friend who complains non-stop.

But NOW you have all the tools necessary to defend your mind, body, and heart against all the sucky things (or people) that may come your way.

Whether it's a negative person, a preep, or that damn fast food cheeseburger—you have the tools and the power to kick those energy vampires to the curb.

So step into your power and say one final goodbye to the sucky thing or person in your life. While they may have sucked your energy before, you no longer have to let it define you. Instead, reclaim your energy and realize how much that person, situation, or thing has made you stronger, cooler, smarter, braver, and the bad-ass gal we always knew you were.

Now, write an ode or one last final goodbye to the sucky person and stand tall in your feminine power!

Dear Sucky Person,

What you did really sucked.

But thanks to that situation you put me in, thing you did, thing you said to me, or the food I ate…I am now a stronger woman.

And I am able to use my newly found power (and energy) to

_____.

Thank you,

_____

—————————————— MOCKTAILS ——————————————

Lemon Cranberry Tonic

   1 cup soda water
   ½ lemon, juiced
   Splash of cranberry juice
   Handful of ice cubes

Directions:
In a shaker or tall glass, combine and shake all ingredients.
Serve immediately.

Minty Kale-oda

   ½ cup fresh kale
   ½ banana
   ½ cup pineapple
   Handful of fresh mint
   ½ lime, peeled
   Handful of ice cubes

Directions:
In a blender, add kale, pineapple, banana, mint, lime and ice.
Process until smooth or creamy. Serve immediately.

— MOCKTAILS —

Sans-gria

Hosting a party? Try serving this non-alcoholic sangria with just a slight caffeine buzz!

   2 cups water
   2 black tea bags
   2 cinnamon sticks
   ¼ cup agave syrup or honey
   3 cups pomegranate juice (can also be any berry juice)
   1 cup freshly squeezed orange juice
   1 orange, sliced into thin rounds
   1 lemon, sliced into thin rounds
   1 lime, sliced into thin rounds
   1 apple, cored and cut into ½ inch chunks
   3 cups sparkling water

Directions:
In a pot, bring water to a boil. Add tea bags and cinnamon sticks and steep for 5 minutes. Discard tea bags and stir in agave to dissolve.

In a large jar or pitcher, combine tea, cinnamon sticks, pomegranate juice, orange juice, orange, lemon, lime, and apple. Refrigerate for at least 1 hour and preferably overnight.
Just before serving, stir in carbonated water. Serve in glasses over ice.

—————————— MOCKTAILS ——————————

Grapefruit Fauxjito

¼ ruby or pink grapefruit, cut into small chunks, seeds removed

2 Tbsp. agave syrup or honey

12 fresh mint leaves, roughly torn

½ cup pink grapefruit soda or flavored mineral water, plus more as needed

mint sprigs, for garnish

Directions:

Put the grapefruit pieces, agave, and mint in a cocktail shaker. Using a muddler, smash the fruit until the juice is released. Add one cup small ice cubes to the shaker with the half cup soda; attach the lid and shake furiously until combined. Divide between two rocks glasses, add more ice if desired, and top off with additional soda. Stir, garnish with mint sprigs and serve.

---------------------- SMOOTHIES ----------------------

The Kickin Ass Smoothie

1 cup kale or spinach

8 pitted sweet bing cherries (Fresh or frozen)

1 banana

1 Tbsp. raw cacao powder

½ cup of unsweetened vanilla almond milk

Directions:
Blend well in blender. Add more ice for a thicker texture. Serve immediately.

Roarin Good Greens Smoothie

1 cup of your choice chopped greens
(Spinach, Kale, Dandelion, or another favorite green)

1 banana

½ cup almond or coconut milk

2-3 ice cubes

Directions:
Blend ingredients and enjoy!

Note: You can add super foods to your smoothie for additional health benefits. Super foods include raw cacao, maca powder, bee pollen, spirulina powder, hemp seed, etc.

—————————————— SMOOTHIES ——————————————

Fierce & Focused Smoothie

1-2 carrots

½ cup cooked or soaked oats

1 Tbsp. cinnamon

1 Tbsp. chia seeds

½ cup unsweetened vanilla almond milk

Directions:
Blend all ingredients and enjoy!

Mood Balancer Smoothie

1 cup raw kale

1 cup blueberries

1 oz. apple cider vinegar

1 Tbsp. raw cacao

½ cup water

Directions:
Blend all ingredients and enjoy!

———————————— SMOOTHIES ————————————

Grounded & Good Smoothie

½ pear

½ banana

½ cup almond milk

1 Tbsp. cinnamon

Handful of ice

Directions:
Blend all ingredients and enjoy!

Strong & Sexy Protein Smoothie

1 scoop plant based protein, chocolate or vanilla
(We love Vega brand!)

½ banana

¼ avocado

½ cup unsweetened coconut milk

Handful of ice

Directions:
Blend all ingredients and enjoy!

——————————— FILLING SNACKS ———————————

Mini Veggie Muffins

1 cup veggies, grated or finely chopped
(whatever you like/have in your refrigerator)

2 eggs, beaten

2 cups quinoa or spelt flour

½ cup parsley, finely chopped

1 cup soy or rice milk

Pinch of sea salt

Directions:

1. Preheat oven to 325 degrees.
2. Mix flour and salt in a bowl.
3. Mix in eggs, veggies and parsley.
4. Mix lightly, gradually add milk. This is supposed to be lumpy so don't work too hard!
5. Spoon into a mini muffin tray that is lightly oiled.
6. Bake for 12-15 minutes.
7. Remove and allow to set for 10 minutes, then serve.

———————— FILLING SNACKS ————————

Tomato and Avocado Salad

1 avocado

1 tomato

2 garlic cloves, minced

¼ cup cilantro, chopped

½ lemon, squeezed

1 Tbsp. olive oil

½ Tb Himalayan sea salt

Directions:

1. Cut and cube avocado and tomato
2. Chop cilantro and add.
3. Mix in lemon, garlic, olive oil and salt.
4. Lightly toss and enjoy!

—————————————— FILLING SNACKS ——————————————

Black Bean and Red Pepper Salad

Ingredients for bean salad:

1 can (16 ounces) black beans, drained and rinsed

1 red bell pepper, diced

1 green pepper, diced

1 cup thinly sliced celery

1 cup thinly sliced green onions

¼ cup fresh cilantro, chopped

Ingredients Cilantro-Cumin Dressing:

⅓ cup olive oil

¼ cup red wine vinegar

1 teaspoon ground cumin

Directions:

1. Combine the beans, peppers, celery, green onions and cilantro in a large mixing bowl.
2. Whisk the oil, vinegar and cumin in a separate smaller bowl.
3. Pour the dressing over the vegetables and stir until thoroughly coated.
4. Let stand 15 minutes to blend the flavors, or refrigerate up to 2 hours before serving.
5. To serve, spoon the salad onto a bed of lettuce or greens.

FILLING SNACKS

Fruit & Nut Soaked Oats

> 1 cup rolled oats
>
> ¼ cup dried fruit
> (such as blueberries, raisins, cranberries, currants)
>
> Handful of almonds
>
> Water

Directions:

1. The night before, place all ingredients in a bowl or mason jar, then fill about ½ inch above oats with water.
2. Cover or seal.
3. Place in a cool, dry place overnight.
4. In the morning, warm with a bit of water over the stove or eat at room temperature.

--------------------- FILLING SNACKS ---------------------

Tsatsiki Dip and Cucumber "Chips"

> 2 cups plain organic Greek yogurt
>
> 1 cup cucumber, diced
>
> 2 garlic cloves, minced
>
> 2 Tbsp. finely chopped dill
>
> 2 Tbsp. fresh lemon juice
>
> Salt and pepper to taste
>
> 1 cucumber, cut into thin slices

Directions:

1. In a bowl combine yogurt, diced cucumber, garlic, dill and lemon.
2. Stir until creamy and season with salt and pepper.
3. Use cucumber slices as "chips."

─────────────── **FILLING SNACKS** ───────────────

Easy Crispy Kale Chips

1 bunch kale

1 Tbsp. olive oil (or olive oil/coconut oil spray)

Salt and pepper to taste

Pinch of cayenne (optional)

Directions:

1. Preheat oven to 350 degrees and line a cookie sheet with tin foil or parchment paper.

2. With a knife or your hands tear away the leaves from the stems and discard stems.

3. Lay torn pieces of kale onto cookie sheet and drizzle or spray with oil and flavor with salt, pepper and cayenne (if you want a kick).

4. Bake until edges are brown but not burnt. About 10-12 minutes.

—————————————— NO BAKE TREATS ——————————

No Bake Bars

> 2 cups pitted dates
>
> 2 cups raw cashews
>
> ½ cup dried blueberries
>
> ¼ cup chia seeds
>
> ½ cup fresh lemon juice

Directions:

1. In food processor, process cashews until they are well ground (not creamy).
2. Then add dates and continue processing until mixture becomes one sticky ball.
3. Mix in dried blueberries, lemon juice and chia seeds.
4. Line a baking pan or sheet with wax paper. Add mixture and press dough firm and evenly.
5. Refrigerate for 30-40 minutes.
6. Remove from fridge and cut into bars. Individually wrap them so you have an easy snack or a delicious breakfast!

———————————— NO BAKE TREATS ————————————

Chunky Monkey Banana Bites

1 banana
Nut Butter
Dark Chocolate Chips

Directions:

1. Slice banana into ½ inch coins.
2. Place one coin down and add a small scoop of nut butter on top.
3. Sprinkle a few chocolate chips on top.
4. Place a banana coin slice on top of the nut butter and chocolate chips. It will look like a little mini sandwich.
5. Enjoy!

Cookie Dough Bites

½ cup almond butter
⅓ cup honey or maple syrup
1 cup almond or cashew flour
¼ cup chocolate chips

1. Combine almond butter and honey or maple syrup.
2. Add the nut flour and mix until a ball of dough forms.
3. Add the chocolate chips.
4. Roll into bite-size balls and freeze for 30 minutes.

———————————— NO BAKE TREATS ————————————

Chocolate Chia Pudding

¼ cup Chia seeds

2 Tbsp. Maple Syrup

1 cup unsweetened almond or coconut milk

2 Tbsp. raw cacao powder

Directions:

1. Combine milk and raw cacao powder in a small mixing bowl and mix until the cacao powder is blended in.
2. Add Chia seeds and maple syrup and mix well.
3. Let chill/set in the fridge for 2-3 hours.
4. Enjoy!

Date Night Bites

2 dates

1 Tbsp. Goat Cheese

4 walnut halves

Directions:

1. Cut each date in half and remove the pit.
2. Stuff each half with goat cheese and top with a walnut half.
3. Enjoy!

Resources

Institute for Integrative Nutrition
www.IntegrativeNutrition.com

Sabre
www.sabrered.com

Rape, Abuse, Incest, National Network (RAINN)
www.rainn.org

The National Domestic Violence Hotline
www.thehotline.org

National Eating Disorder Association
www.NationalEatingDisorders.org

The Joyful Heart Foundation
www.JoyfulHeartFoundation.org

World Martial Arts Center
www.happykicks.com

Websites We Love

www.MindBodyGreen.com
www.PositivelyPositive.com
www.TheDailyLove.com
www.UpWorthy.com
www.KidPresident.com

Foods We Love

Vega

Larabar

NibMor Chocolate

Rise Bars

Zola Coconut Water

Brad's Raw

Mary's Gone Crackers

Manitoba Harvest

Hail Merry

Brands We Love

Aerie

Dona Jo Fitwear

Affirmats

Empower Fitness

Books We Love

A Return to Love by Marianne Williamson

Junk Foods & Junk Moods by Lindsey Smith

The Bliss Cleanse by Lorraine Miller and Lindsey Smith

From Gratitude to Bliss by Lorraine Miller

The Gift of Fear by Gavin de Becker

Excuses Begone! by Wayne Dyer

Integrative Nutrition by Joshua Rosenthal

Food Rules by Michael Pollan

The Five Love Languages by Gary Chapman

The Way of the Peaceful Warrior by Dan Millman
The Power of Now by Eckhart Tolle
How to Win Friends and Influence People by Dale Carnegie

Videos We Love

Stilettos and Self Defense, Volumes 1-3
Miss Representation
Brave Miss World
Food, Inc.
Supersize Me
Forks Over Knives
Fed Up

About Jennifer

Jennifer was 23 years old when she swung her first sword in a HapKiDo class in NYC. For the first time in her life she felt strong, safe and sexy and she wanted to share that feeling with every woman.

Today she's a clinical nutritionist, fitness expert and 3rd degree black belt who travels the world working with global business leaders and creating corporate wellness programs. She received her nutrition training at the Institute for Integrative Nutrition and later received a Master's degree in Clinical Nutrition at the University of Bridgeport.

She's been featured on The Doctors, Bethenny and Marie Osmond and even taught Princess Leia (Carrie Fisher), self-defense on The Today Show. She's been published on The Huffington Post and blogs for Livestrong.com as well as her own website. You can find her health advice in numerous publications like Women's Health, Marie Claire and Fitness.

Jenny McCarthy described her as "one kick ass, bad ass chick."

When she's not teaching women to kick butt, consulting on corporate projects, writing, or globe trotting with her VIP clients, you can find her at the gym, on a hike, on a bike or enjoying healthy-ish meals with her friends and loved ones.

Meet her over at www.jennifercassetta.com.

About Lindsey

When Lindsey was 12 years old, she had a panic attack that sent her into the hospital.

After that experience, she committed herself to health and happiness, by self-seeking coaches and mentors. And within a few years, Lindsey starting teaching her own stress management classes to her high school peers.

And let's just say—the rest is history.

As an author and speaker, she's deeply passionate about helping others live a healthy and happy life.

One reader described her as a "young spirit rocking an old soul," while another declared her to be the "next generation Arianna Huffington."

Her stories and tips have been featured on the Liza Oz Show, MindBodyGreen and CBS News. She is also one of the leading contributors on Ehow.com.

When she's not drinking kale smoothies, you can find her writing, speaking and rapping about self-love.

Meet Lindsey and stay in-the-know about her upcoming happenings at www.FoodMoodGirl.com.

Book a Hear Me Roar Workshop!

Hear Me Roar is a funny, engaging and hands-on presentation that gives young women tools to be confident and safe in any situation. The workshop is taught by Lindsey Smith, a certified health coach, published author and rape survivor, and Jennifer Cassetta, a 3rd degree black belt, nutritionist and personal safety expert. The two are a powerful combination that inspire and empower young women to kick butt in all areas of their life.

Here are 5 great reasons why your college or university needs to host a Hear Me Roar workshop this fall:

1. 1 in 3 women globally will be the victim of a sexual assault in their lifetime.

2. College-age girls are 4 times more likely than the general population to be a victim of rape, attempted rape or sexual assault.

3. Because even our President thinks that college campuses can be doing a better job at raising awareness around sexual assault prevention.

4. Hear Me Roar is a dynamic and fun way to raise awareness around a serious subject.

5. If you prevent just 1 girl from getting raped on your campus, this workshop…is priceless.

Hear What Workshop Attendees Are Saying:

Hear Me Roar is unlike any workshop I've experienced. Jennifer and Lindsey are highly skilled in their areas of expertise AND they teach a heavy subject matter in a FUN way.

This is a MUST HAVE program for EVERY college campus nationwide!

- Aire, attendee

Hear Me Roar was a great opportunity for the Robert Morris sororities to bond over being powerful women! We learned how to protect ourselves and now we can spread the word to other girls. Did I mention we had a BLAST?!

- Caralee Russell
Robert Morris University

For more information or to book a workshop, contact info@promotingnaturalhealth.com

ROARIN' REVIEWS

"Some people suck. This book...does not. Martial arts moves...scripts to say NO to a creep...tips for online safety...and a list of all the things in your purse that can be used as a weapon... um, hello! For women who want to be strong, safe and sexy — out there in a world that can sometimes be lame, scary + sucky — this book's got it all."

- Alexandra Franzen
  Best-Selling Author

"Hear Me Roar is just the wakeup call many young women need! The numbers speak for themselves. Assaults are happening and educating yourself about how to feel empowered and in control is something SABRE is proud to support."

- David Nance
  Personal Safety Expert &
  SABRE CEO

"Hear Me Roar guides women of all ages to become healthy, happy, strong, confident and ready to take on the world!"

- Joshua Rosenthal
  Founder of the Institute for
  Integrative Nutrition

"Weakness and meekness is not an option on the road to success and womanhood! Jennifer and Lindsey help guide young ladies with practical, strong, advice along the bumpy road of life which is full of sucky people."

- Karla Cavalli
  TV Host

"Hear Me Roar will make you feel like a rockstar ready to kick ass and take on the world. Do yourself a favor and grab a copy immediately!"

- Sharzad Kiadeh
  Internet Personality